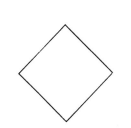

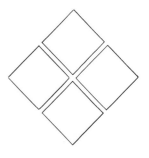

I$\frac{R}{P}$ INFORMATION RESOURCES PRESS, WASHINGTON, D.C., 1973

A Guide
to Sources of
Consumer Information

by Sarah M. Thomas
and Bernadine Weddington

With a Foreword by Virginia H. Knauer

Available from Information Resources Press
2100 M Street, N.W., Washington, D.C. 20037

Library of Congress Catalog Card Number 73-77342
ISBN 0-87815-010-2

Foreword

I believe our educational systems have too often missed their great opportunity to provide consumer education to our young people. Students are taught how to earn a living, but few have been taught how to buy or how to protect themselves against fraudulent practices. Add to this the tragic fact that nearly 45 percent of men and women over 25 have never finished high school, and what we have is a grand sum of consumer illiteracy.

The net result of consumer illiteracy is too often ruined budgets, ruined marriages, failures to shop wisely for a given product, and susceptibility to deceptive schemes.

We have been able to make some inroads against consumer illiteracy. In addition to the *Consumer Education Biblography* published by my Office of Consumer Affairs, my office has published *Suggested Guidelines for Consumer Education, Kindergarten Through Twelfth Grade.*

This guideline has been sent to every school system in the country, and we are seeing an increasing number of schools add consumer courses to their curriculum. Now we are developing adult education guidelines, with emphasis on special socioeconomic groups.

We also publish a *Guide to Federal Consumer Services* to inform consumers about the services and information that are available to them from the Federal Government.

But much more can be done. That is why I am pleased that Sarah M. Thomas and Bernadine Weddington have compiled A *Guide to Sources of Consumer Information.* Educators, libraries, students, and citizens can find within this compilation many useful books and reference materials.

These works are not only cures for a disease, but an important ingredient in a health marketplace. Imagine what would happen if we could turn the present statistics around; if we could say that most of our citizens are properly informed about goods and services.

Would the gypster flourish as he too often does now? Wouldn't manufacturers be more willing to give out information on the quality of their products, rather than—as they too often do now—irrelevant sales appeals?

We need this *Guide to Sources of Consumer Information* just as we need other excellent works on topics which make up the broad umbrella of consumerism.

Virginia H. Knauer
SPECIAL ASSISTANT TO THE PRESIDENT
FOR CONSUMER AFFAIRS

Preface

◇ The right to make an intelligent choice among products and services.

◇ The right to accurate information with which to make a free choice.

◇ The right to expect that the health and safety of the buyer is taken into account by those who seek his patronage.

◇ The right to register dissatisfaction, and have a complaint heard and weighed, when a buyer's interests are badly served.

This is what President Nixon envisaged as the concept of buyers' rights in his executive order establishing the Office of Consumer Affairs.

For many years, there have been laws protecting the consumer, but he has been unaware of them. Now, federal, state, and local governments are publicizing these laws and enacting more as the need arises. Consumer groups have been organized to inform the consumer about these laws and to help him obtain redress from unjust or illegal practices.

In recent years, interest in consumer affairs has been spurred by Ralph Nader and other consumer advocates, both in and out of government. Increased awareness has brought about a demand for specific information to aid the consumer and has resulted in increased activities to provide this information.

The purpose of this *Guide* is to provide the reader with sources of information *for* the consumer, rather than information *about* the consumer. The *Guide* is divided into two parts: I – Published Information and II – Organizations.

Part I – Published Information includes books, directories, documents, periodicals, and indexes published in the United States since 1960. This material was obtained through extensive literature searches at the Library of Congress, the University of Maryland Library, the University of North Carolina at Chapel Hill Library, the Montgomery County (Maryland) Libraries, the Cumberland County (North Carolina) Library and of published indexing and abstracting services and specialized bibliographies and newsletters.

Part II – Organizations contains descriptions of federal, state, and local government and private groups concerned with consumer affairs that provide both published and unpublished materials. Except for mere listings, this information was obtained directly from the groups named. Films and other audiovisual materials have been listed under the organizations offering them.

Undoubtedly, many items that should have been included have been overlooked; many have been included that should have been omitted. No effort has been made to judge the quality of the material listed. The single criterion for inclusion was that the sources provide information useful to the consumer. Comments and suggestions are welcome.

As a result of rapid developments in consumer information sources, there may be some changes made in publications, services, or prices described in this book before it reaches print. However, we have attempted to provide the most current information possible under the circumstances.

Appreciation is extended to all the individuals and organizations who contributed to making this *Guide* possible, and to Nettie T. Clark, who assisted in the typing of the manuscript.

Contents

Acknowledgements

Figure 1 is reprinted by permission from *Changing Times*, the Kiplinger Magazine (January 1972 issue). Copyright 1972 by The Kiplinger Washington Editors, Inc., 1729 H Street, N.W., Washington, D.C. 20006. Figure 2 is reprinted by permission from *Changing Times*, the Kiplinger Magazine (July 1972 issue). Copyright 1972 by The Kiplinger Washington Editors, Inc., 1729 H Street, N.W., Washington, D.C. 20006. Figure 3, reprinted from the *Consumer Bulletin*, and Figure 4, reprinted from *Consumer Bulletin Annual*, are used by kind permission of Consumers' Research, Inc. Figure 5 is reproduced by kind permission of the Chamber of Commerce of the United States. Figure 6 is reproduced by permission of H. Morris of Budget Gadget. Figure 7 is reproduced by kind permission of the Chamber of Commerce of the United States.

Published Information

A Guides to Information
B Textbooks and Consumer Education Materials
C General Interest
D Periodicals

Published Information

Much information is available to consumers through published literature. As the need for consumer education increases, the need for bibliographies, guides to the literature, directories, educational materials, and popularly written items will increase. This part of the *Guide* attempts to provide a listing of these materials, arranged primarily by user groups.

Directory A covers guides to published and unpublished information in the form of bibliographies; directories; indexing and abstracting services; and guides to new publications, publications in specific subject areas, and reviews. Primary users of this Directory will be researchers, librarians, teachers, students, individuals actively involved in the consumer movement, and those seeking a specific kind of information.

Directory B—of primary use to curriculum developers, teachers, and researchers—is devoted to textbooks and other consumer education materials for consumers of all interest levels.

Directory C contains information of general interest, often popular-type reading material. The items listed offer information on one or many aspects of consumer affairs and often lead to additional sources of information through bibliographies, charts and tables, special listings, and appendixes.

Directory D includes listings of periodicals in the field of consumer affairs and those containing features or irregular coverage.

The materials discussed should be available at public or local college and university libraries.

Guides to Information

As consumer problems increase, the need for information about these problems and their possible solutions also increases. More and more attention is being directed to alerting the consumer to bad business practices; more and more activities are being set up to handle complaints at all levels of government and the private sector. But the consumer still is left with the complex problem of sorting all this information for his own use, that is, knowing how to register a complaint, knowing the implications of new laws and regulations as they relate to him, and similar questions. The consumer wants—and needs—simple answers to his day-to-day problems; for example, which food products to buy, how much to pay for a product, how to select a doctor or lawyer, how to avoid being cheated when borrowing money, and how to go about buying a home.

Since the consumer will very often seek the aforementioned information at libraries and from educational programs, the librarians, teachers, and others who select such information must attempt to provide complete coverage of the various types of consumer materials that are suitable to the many different levels of users—often in several languages.

The published material listed in Directory A was selected to provide both these groups—the individual consumer and librarians and teachers—with the means to identify and obtain needed information to answer specific questions that concern consumers. In most cases, these publications will not provide specific answers, but will lead to other sources that will.

3

A1   AMERICAN BOOK PUBLISHING RECORD   New York, R.R. Bowker, 1960– . Monthly. $19/year.
Guide to new books, arranged by subject in Dewey Decimal number order. Contains author and title indexes.

A2   AMERICAN LIBRARY DIRECTORY   New York, R.R. Bowker, 1918–1919– . Biennial. $25.
Guide to public, special, college, and university libraries in the United States and Canada. Arrangement is geographical by state (or province) and city and, within each location, by name of library.

A3   ANNUAL LIST OF ACCREDITED HOSPITALS   Chicago, Joint Commission on Accreditation of Hospitals, 1953. Annual; updated quarterly. $3.

A4   ANNUAL LIST OF ACCREDITED LONG-TERM CARE FACILITIES   Chicago, Joint Commission on Accreditation of Hospitals, 1953. Annual; updated quarterly. $3.

A5   AYER DIRECTORY OF PUBLICATIONS   (Formerly *Directory of Newspapers and Periodicals*) Philadelphia, Ayer Press, 1869– . Annual. $42.
Annual directory of American newspapers (dailies, weeklies, and monthlies) and magazines in the consumer, business, technical, trade, and farm fields.

A6   BEST'S RECOMMENDED INSURANCE ADJUSTERS 1972   42nd Edition. Morristown, N.J., A.M. Best, 1972. Annual.
Lists recommended adjusters; arranged geographically.

A7   BEST'S RECOMMENDED INSURANCE ATTORNEYS WITH DIGEST OF INSURANCE LAWS, 1971–72   43rd Edition. Morristown, N.J., A.M. Best, 1972. Annual. $10.
Lists (geographically by state and city) individuals and firms, specialties (if any), addresses and telephone numbers, partners, and clients.

A8 **BIBLIOGRAPHIC INDEX; A Cumulative Bibliography of Bibliographies** Bronx, N.Y., H.W. Wilson, 1937– . Triannual in April, August, and December. Sold on service basis.
Alphabetical subject arrangement of bibliographies published separately and those published as parts of books and journals. Includes such areas as consumer credit, consumer education, and consumer protection.

A9 **BIBLIOGRAPHY OF AGRICULTURE** U.S. National Agricultural Library. New York, CCM Information Corporation, 1942– . $85.00/year; with annual cumulation, $137.50.
Bibliography, arranged by subject classification, covering the current literature received by the National Agricultural Library. Includes food and human nutrition, home economics, consumer foods, consumer education, and consumer protection.

A10 **BIBLIOGRAPHY OF RESEARCH ON CONSUMER AND HOMEMAKING EDUCATION** By Anna Marguriette and Joel H. Magisos. Columbus, Ohio, Clearinghouse on Vocational and Technical Education, Ohio State University, 1970. $3.29 (microfiche $0.65).
Bibliography of research in consumer and home economics education, wage-earning economics, and other research areas of less interest to consumers.

A11 **BIOLOGICAL AND AGRICULTURAL INDEX** (Formerly *Agricultural Index*) Bronx, N.Y., H.W. Wilson, 1948– . Monthly except August, with annual cumulations. Sold on service basis.
A cumulative subject index to English-language periodicals in the fields of biology, agriculture, and related sciences. Consumer education and consumer protection also are covered.

A12 **BUSINESS PERIODICALS INDEX** Bronx, N.Y., H.W. Wilson, 1958– . Monthly except August. Sold on service basis.
A cumulative subject index to business periodicals published in the English language. Coverage includes consumer credit,

5

durable goods, consumer education, finance companies, consumer panels, consumer protection, consumer cooperatives, unit pricing, food additives, and food laws and regulations.

A13 **CATALOG OF FEDERAL DOMESTIC ASSISTANCE** Washington, D.C., Office of Management and Budget, 1968– . Annual. $6.75.

Describes and explains the purpose of the Federal Government's domestic programs, tells where to apply for them, and lists printed materials available.

A14 **CIS/INDEX TO PUBLICATIONS OF THE UNITED STATES CONGRESS** Washington, D.C., Congressional Information Service, 1970– . Monthly. Price based on size of book and periodical budget.

Monthly list of hearings, reports, committee prints, and other congressional papers, with abstracts. Also contains indexes by subject, name, bill number, report number, document number, and committee and subcommittee chairmen.

A15 **CQ WEEKLY REPORT** Washington, D.C., Congressional Quarterly, Inc., 1945– . Weekly; indexed quarterly and annually. $144/year.

Covers current congressional activities and includes brief articles, tables, and fact sheets.

A16 **CONGRESSIONAL STAFF DIRECTORY** Edited by Charles B. Brownson. Washington, D.C., Congressional Staff Directory, 1959– . Annual. $13.50.

A directory of the legislative and executive branches. Includes such information as congressional members and staffs, titles, locations, and telephone numbers; committee and subcommittee assignments; district and state offices of members of Congress; biographies of members and data on districts represented; and key personnel of executive departments.

A17 **CONSUMER DIRECTORY** Columbus, Mo., American Council on Consumer Interests, 1967. $2.

Includes names, addresses, and biographical information of persons with a professional interest in consumer affairs.

A18 **CONSUMER EDUCATION BIBLIOGRAPHY; Prepared for the President's Committee on Consumer Interests by the Yonkers Public Library** Washington, D.C., U.S. Government Printing Office, 1969. $0.65.

Contains "over 2,000 books, booklets, pamphlets, files, film-strips, etc., in the field of consumer interests and education . . ." Includes a list of agencies and organizations that provide services to consumers. Consumer goods and services—purchases and use—and various consumer problems such as credit, fraud, and money management are covered. The last section is devoted to methods and materials for consumer education.

A19 **CONSUMER LAW BIBLIOGRAPHY** Compiled by Richard A. Elbrecht. Brighton, Mass., National Consumer Law Center, Boston College Law School, 1971. Publication number A044.550. $4.

Arranged by subject; covers contracts, warranties, and other matters of interest to the consumer.

A20 **CUMULATIVE BOOK INDEX: A World List of Books in the English Language** Bronx, N.Y., H.W. Wilson, 1928– Monthly except August. Sold on service basis.

Cumulative listing of English-language books, arranged alphabetically by subject, author, and title. Includes a list of publishers and addresses.

A21 **CURRENT INDEX TO JOURNALS IN EDUCATION** New York, CCM Information Corporation, 1969– . Monthly, with semiannual and annual cumulations. $39/year.

Detailed monthly index to more than 300 education and education-oriented journals. Companion to *Research in Education*, indexed by the same headings. Includes main entry section with author and subject indexes. Coverage includes consumer economics and consumer education.

7

A22 DEVELOPING A RESOURCE CENTER IN CONSUMER EDUCATION: AN ANNOTATED BIBLIOGRAPHY Compiled by Thomas Garman, Floyd L. Crank, and Julienne V. Cochran. De Kalb, Ill., Northern Illinois University, Business Education Department, 1971. $2.

More than 1,300 entries for audiovisual materials, divided into 18 subject areas. Includes a listing of 100 consumer periodicals (with addresses) offering free or inexpensive materials.

A23 DIRECTORY OF AMERICAN SAVINGS AND LOAN ASSOCIATIONS Baltimore, T.K. Sanderson, 1955– . Annual. $30.

Annual compilation of savings and loan associations, arranged by state and city, with sections on Federal Home Loan Banks and Cooperative Banks. Entries include addresses, telephone numbers, officers, membership, assets, and branches. A direct reduction loan amortization schedule is included in the *Directory*.

A24 DIRECTORY OF GOVERNMENT AGENCIES SAFEGUARDING CONSUMER AND ENVIRONMENT 4th Edition. Alexandria, Va., Serina Press, 1972. Biennial. $5.95.

Provides listings of federal and state agencies with jurisdiction over food and drugs, dangerous drugs, meats, pesticides, fraud and deceptive practices, and insurance. Poison Control Centers, consumer specialists in FDA district offices, and consumer representatives in some state, county, and city governments also are given. Arranged alphabetically by state; subject; and state, federal, and regional offices.

A25 DIRECTORY OF INFORMATION RESOURCES IN AGRICULTURE AND BIOLOGY Beltsville, Md., National Agricultural Library, 1971. $4.50.

A directory of federal organizations, units of land-grant colleges and universities, and campus-affiliated organizations that was developed as an aid to the Agricultural Science Information Network Development Plan. Coverage includes agriculture and home economics. Arranged by state, with Organization and

Bibliographic and Collections indexes. Also includes a subject index of Prime Research Areas.

A26 A DIRECTORY OF INFORMATION RESOURCES IN THE UNITED STATES: Federal Government Library of Congress, National Referral Center for Science and Technology. Washington, D.C., U.S. Government Printing Office, 1967. $2.75.
Includes sources of information on consumer credit, education and protection, financial affairs, products, and research in the Federal Government.

A27 DIRECTORY OF LEGAL AID AND DEFENDER SERVICES, 1971 National Legal Aid and Defender Association. Chicago, American Bar Center, 1971. $3.50.
Contains names, addresses, and descriptions of services provided by each group.

A28 DIRECTORY OF SPECIAL LIBRARIES AND INFORMATION CENTERS Edited by Anthony T. Kruzas. 2nd Edition. Detroit, Gale Research, 1968. 2 Vols. Vol. 1 – Special Libraries and Information Centers in the United States and Canada, $28.50; Vol. 2 – Geographic-Personnel Index to Special Libraries, $23.50.
Volume 1 is arranged alphabetically by name of library or center, with subject index by library specialization. Each entry includes address and phone number, date founded, number of staff members, major subject areas covered, size of collection, publications, and services. Volume 2, arranged in two sections, contains geographic and personnel indexes.

A29 DIRECTORY OF URBAN AFFAIRS INFORMATION AND RESEARCH CENTERS Compiled by Eric V.A. Winston. Metuchen, N.J., Scarecrow, 1970. $5.
A listing of more than 200 organizations, agencies, and institutions active in combating urban ills.

A30 EDUCATIONAL MEDIA INDEX Educational Media Council. New York, McGraw-Hill, 1964. 14 Vols. $62.45/set.

Multivolume guide to film strips, phonotapes, slides or transparencies, models and mock-ups, flat pictures, film or kinescope, phonodiscs, videotape, cross-media kits, charts and maps, and programmed instructional material. Volume 8 ($4.70), *Health-Safety and Home Economics*, covers home management, clothing, and foods. Indexed materials are for use by grade seven through college and adult levels. A separate title index to each section and a source address list appear at the end of this volume.

A31   **EDUCATION INDEX**   Bronx, N.Y., H.W. Wilson, 1929– . Monthly except July and August. Sold on service basis.

Contains author and subject indexes to a selected list of educational periodicals, proceedings, yearbooks, bulletins, monographs, and material printed by the U.S. Government. Coverage includes consumer education, consumers and consumer preferences, credit, and home economics.

A32   **ENCYCLOPEDIA OF ASSOCIATIONS**   7th Edition. Detroit, Gale Research, 1972. 2 Vols. Vol. 1 – $38.50; Vol. 2 – $25.00.

A directory of national associations in the United States, with geographic and executive indexes. Trade and business, governmental, social welfare, educational, and cultural associations are arranged by subject area with a keyword index. Entries for each association include location, size, officers, objectives, and publications. A supplement which updates the *Encyclopedia* is available.

A33   **ENCYCLOPEDIA OF BUSINESS INFORMATION SOURCES: A Detailed Listing of Primary Subjects of Interest to Managerial Personnel, with a Record of Sourcebooks, Periodicals, Organizations, Directories, Handbooks, Bibliographies, and Other Sources of Information on Each Topic.** 2nd Edition. Detroit, Gale Research, 1970. 2 Vols. $47.50/set.

The first volume is arranged by subject; the second by geographic location. Of interest to the consumer are sections on consumer credit, consumer education, finance companies, consumer price indexes, consumer surveys, consumers, quality of products, cooperative movements, banks and banking, trademarks and trade names, and various types of insurance.

A34 **ENCYCLOPEDIA OF UNITED STATES GOVERN-MENT BENEFITS** Edited by Roy A. Grisham, Jr. and Paul D. McConaughy. Union City, N.J., William H. Wise and Company, 1967. $12.95.
Guide to available U.S. Government benefits. Reference catalog of services with details of eligibility. Arranged alphabetically by benefit classification with numerous cross-references.

A35 **FILM REVIEW INDEX** Edited by Wesley A. Doak and William J. Speed. Monterey, Calif., Audio-Visual Associates, 1972– . Quarterly. $30/year.
Each quarterly index of film reviews contains the name of the film, source of the review, volume, issue, page, date, and reviewer's name.

A36 **FOOD INDUSTRY SOURCEBOOK, Consumerism-Environmentalism: Issues, Actions, Reactions, Information for Communication** Washington, D.C., National Canners Association, 1970. $20.
A guide to information sources of specific interest to the food processing industry. Listings are divided into the following sections: government, education, consumerism, environmentalism, industry, publications, and journalists. A statement of consumer functions, how these are performed and enforced, laws administered, and how to obtain services is provided for each federal agency. Names and addresses are provided for state governmental agencies in order to obtain specific types of available information.

A37 **FREE AND INEXPENSIVE EDUCATIONAL AIDS** By Thomas J. Pepe. 3rd Edition, Rev. New York, Dover Publ., 1966. $1.75.
Lists 1,700 books, films, booklets, charts, posters, and slides in areas of agriculture; arts, crafts, and hobbies; health and hygiene; homes and homemaking; materials, processes, and

products; safety; and nutrition and diet. Includes a list of companies with addresses, an index of audiovisual aids, and a general index.

A38 **FREE AND INEXPENSIVE LEARNING MATERIALS** 5th Edition. Nashville, George Peabody College for Teachers, Division of Surveys and Field Services, 1970. $3.
Arranged by topic headings or areas of study. Includes consumer credit and consumer problems.

A39 **GEBBIE PRESS HOUSE MAGAZINE DIRECTORY: A Public Relations and Free Lance Guide to the Nation's Leading House Magazines** New York, Gebbie Press, 1952– . Triennial. $24.95.
Includes names of editors, company names, magazine titles, frequency of publication, and subject interests. Arranged alphabetically with title and geographic indexes. Coverage includes food, home appliances, home furnishings, and new products.

A40 **GOVERNMENT REPORTS INDEX** Springfield, Va., National Technical Information Service, 1965– . Semimonthly. $22/year.
Provides indexes to reports of federally sponsored research and development announced in *Government Reports Announcements* ($30/year) by subject, personal author, corporate author, contract number, and accession/report number. Consumer education and protection are among the subjects covered.

A41 **GUIDE TO AMERICAN DIRECTORIES** Edited by Bernard Klein. 8th Edition. Rye, N.Y., B. Klein Publ., 1972. $30.
A guide to the major business directories of the United States, covering all industrial, professional, and mercantile categories. It is designed primarily to assist organizations, associations, and those engaged in advertising, market research, and public relations in finding current, reliable sources of information. Arranged by subject category, coverage includes consumer information, finance companies, food industries, and insurance.

A42   GUIDE TO FEDERAL CONSUMER SERVICES Executive Office of the President, Office of Consumer Affairs. Washington, D.C., U.S. Government Printing Office, 1971. $1.

A revised and updated guide to government programs and services. For each office listed, information is provided on organizational structure, purpose, laws administered, major functions for consumers, how these are performed, how to obtain them, and publications and their availability.

A43   GUIDE TO MICROFORMS IN PRINT Edited by Albert J. Diaz. Washington, D.C., National Cash Register, Microcard Editions, 1961– . Annual. $4.

Cumulative guide to books, journals, and other materials available in microform. Books are entered by author, journals by title, and newspapers by state and city.

A44   GUIDE TO MODERN MEDICAL CARE By S.D. Klotz. New York, Scribner's, 1967. $6.95.

Practical guide to choosing a doctor, hospital, health insurance company, psychiatrist, dentist, or pharmacist, with an annotated bibliography and a glossary. Appendixes include lists of American Specialty Boards, Health and Medical Organizations, National Voluntary Health Organizations, and Laboratory and Radiologic charges.

A45   INDEX TO 16-MM EDUCATIONAL FILMS National Information Center for Education Media, University of Southern California. 2nd Edition. New York, R.R. Bowker, 1969. $29.50.

Lists films available for use in consumer education programs related to home management.

A46   INDEX TO 35-MM EDUCATIONAL FILMSTRIPS National Information Center for Education Media, University of Southern California. 2nd Edition. New York, R.R. Bowker, 1970. $34.

A companion volume to *Index to 16-mm Educational Films*. Includes listings for consumer education under Home Economics-Home Management.

A47 **INSURANCE ALMANAC** New York, Underwriter Printing Publ., 1970. $20.

Who, what, when, and where in insurance. Annual directory of agents and brokers, adjusters, organizations, state officials, management groups, insurance groups, mutual property companies, accident and health insurance companies, and life insurance companies. Includes general index by name of company.

A48 **MONTHLY CHECKLIST OF STATE PUBLICATIONS** Library of Congress. Washington, D.C., U.S. Government Printing Office, 1910– . Monthly. $8/year.

Lists state documents issued during the past five years that have been received by the Library of Congress. Includes monographs and series, periodicals, publications of associations of state officials and regional organizations, studies, manuals, and statistical reports. Covers subjects such as consumer credit, education, and protection.

A49 **NATIONAL DIRECTORY OF NEWSLETTERS AND REPORTING SERVICES: A Reference Guide to National, International, and Selected Foreign Newsletters, Information Services, Financial Services, Association Bulletins, Training and Educational Services** Detroit, Gale Research, 1966. $20.

Broad subject arrangement of more than 1,500 newsletters and reporting services. Each entry includes title, publisher, address, frequency of publication, editor's name, and subjects covered. Provides title, subject, and publisher indexes.

A50 **THE NEW HANDBOOK OF PRESCRIPTION DRUGS** By Richard Burack. New York, Random House, 1970. $7.95.

Guide to official names of drugs with prices and sources.

A51 **NEW YORK TIMES INDEX** New York, New York Times, 1913– . Semimonthly, with annual cumulations. $87.50; annual cumulation, $87.50; both, $150.00.

Subject index with date, page, and column. A brief synopsis of the article also is given.

A52 **P.A.I.S. (Public Affairs Information Service) BULLETIN**
New York, P.A.I.S., Inc., 1952– . Weekly. $100/year.
Listing of current books, pamphlets, periodical articles, and
government documents in the fields of economics and public
affairs. Arranged by subjects such as consumer cooperative
movements, consumer credit, charge accounts, debt, finance
companies, installment plans, durable goods, consumer goods,
consumer panels, and consumer protection.

A53 **POLK'S WORLD BANK DIRECTORY—NORTH AMER-
ICAN SECTION** 154th Edition. Nashville, R.L. Polk, 1818– .
Semiannual, with supplements. $52.50/year.
Alphabetical listing of all banks in the United States and its
territories, arranged by states and territories, by cities within
each state, and then by banks within each city. Each entry
includes name and address, telephone number, date of establishment, kind of bank and association memberships, officers,
branches, stocks, assets, and liabilities.

A54 **A POPULAR GUIDE TO GOVERNMENT PUBLICA-
TIONS** By William Philip Leidy. 3rd Edition. New York,
Columbia University Press, 1968. $12.
Includes selections from the *Monthly Catalog, United States
Government Publications* and popular titles of the Pan American Union published between 1961 and mid-1966. Entries are
grouped according to broad subject areas. Appendixes list field
offices of the U.S. Department of Commerce and other departments and agencies from which material may be obtained free
of charge or by direct purchase. Also provides a subject index.

A55 **RAND McNALLY INTERNATIONAL BANK DIREC-
TORY** Chicago, Rand McNally, 1872– . Semiannual. $45.
Directory of banks and bankers.

A56 **READER'S GUIDE TO PERIODICAL LITERATURE**
New York, H.W. Wilson, 1905– . Semimonthly; monthly in
July and August. $32.

Subject and author indexes to periodicals of general interest published in the United States. Coverage includes consumer credit, credit cards, commercial products, consumer education, consumer protection, Better Business Bureaus, food, and consumer surveys.

A57 **SERVICE DIRECTORY OF NATIONAL ORGANIZA-TIONS, 1971** New York, National Assembly, 1971. $8.

Outlines purposes, programs, services, and organizational structures for the major national health, welfare, and recreational agencies, both governmental and voluntary. Contains information on where and how to apply for services.

A58 **SOCIAL SCIENCES AND HUMANITIES INDEX** New York, H.W. Wilson, 1916– . Sold on service basis.

An author and subject index to periodicals in the fields of economics, sociology, and related subjects. Subjects of interest to the consumer are consumer protection, boycott, consumer credit, and consumer products.

A59 **SOURCES OF AUDIO-VISUAL MATERIALS** By Milbrey Jones. Washington, D.C., U.S. Government Printing Office, 1967. OE-35000. $0.15.

Includes listings of audio-visual materials and of periodicals that review audio-visual materials for elementary and secondary school levels.

A60 **SOURCES OF BUSINESS INFORMATION** By Edwin T. Coman, Jr. Berkeley, University of California Press, 1965. $8.50.

A guide to basic sources of information on firms and individuals, financial services, real estate, and insurance, among other topics. Includes bibliographies, handbooks, yearbooks, trade magazines, books, and magazines in the subject area.

A61 **SOURCES OF INFORMATION IN THE SOCIAL SCIENCES: A Guide to the Literature** By Carl M. White. Totowa, N.J., Bedminster Press, 1964. $10.50.

Lists sources of information under broad subject headings

such as economics and business administration, sociology, and education. Includes sources of unpublished information in addition to handbooks, manuals, compendia, journals, organizations, bibliographies, encyclopedias, and directories.

A62   **SOURCES OF MEDICAL INFORMATION; A Guide to Organizations and Government Agencies Which Are Sources of Information in Fields of Medicine, Health, Disease, Drugs, Mental Health, and Related Areas, and to Currently Available Pamphlets, Reprints and Selected Scientific Papers**   Edited by Raphael Alexander. New York, Exceptional Books, 1969. $4.50.

     Lists organizations and publications under broad subject categories. A general list of sources of publications is included at the end of the book. One complete chapter is devoted to fraud and quackery.

A63   **STANDARD PERIODICAL DIRECTORY**   Edited by Leon Garry. 3rd Edition. New York, Oxbridge Publ., 1964. Annual. $25.

     A complete guide to more than 20,000 U.S. and Canadian periodicals: industrial, business, medical, farm, scientific, scholarly, technical, legal, general interest, arts and humanities, trade, government, social sciences, newsletters, financial services, literary, house organs, directories, political, annuals, and engineering. Arranged alphabetically by subject, with author and subject indexes.

A64   **SUBJECT GUIDE TO BOOKS IN PRINT: An Index to the Publishers' Trade List Annual**   New York, R.R. Bowker, 1957– . Annual. $23.50.

     Titles listed in *Books in Print* are indexed by subject category. Included are books on consumer credit, education, protection, and other subjects of interest to consumers.

A65   **SUBJECT GUIDE TO FORTHCOMING BOOKS; A Bi-Monthly Subject Forecast of Books to Come**   New York, R.R. Bowker, 1967– . Bimonthly. $8.75.

     Broad subject arrangement of books scheduled for publication. Subject index, by author and title, to titles listed in *Forthcoming Books.*

A66 **SUBJECT GUIDE TO MAJOR UNITED STATES GOVERNMENT PUBLICATIONS** Chicago, American Library Association, 1968. $5.50.

Comprehensive guide to publications issued by the U.S. Government Printing Office. Coverage includes bankruptcies, food, family income, prices, weights, and measures.

A67 **SUBJECT GUIDE TO MICROFORMS IN PRINT** Edited by Albert J. Diaz. Washington, D.C., National Cash Register, Microcard Editions, 1962– . Annual. $6.

A listing, by subject, of printed materials available in microform. Banking, insurance, and home economics are among the subjects of interest to consumers.

A68 **ULRICH'S INTERNATIONAL PERIODICALS DIRECTORY; A Classified Guide to a Selected List of Current Periodicals, Foreign and Domestic** New York, R.R. Bowker, 1932 . Biennial. 2 Vols. $42.50/set.

Titles are listed alphabetically by subject. Each entry includes title, sponsoring organization, frequency of publication, editors, price, publisher, and place of publication.

A69 **UNITED STATES GOVERNMENT ORGANIZATION MANUAL** General Services Administration, National Archives and Records Service, Office of the Federal Register. Washington, D.C., U.S. Government Printing Office, 1935– . Annual. $3.

Official handbook of the Federal Government. Contains a brief description of each agency and includes a section entitled "Sources of Information."

A70 **UNITED STATES GOVERNMENT SERIALS AND PERIODICALS** Edited by John L. Andriot. McLean, Va., Documents Index, 1971. 3 Vols. $60/set.

Lists publications of existing as well as defunct agencies. Provides agency, subject, and title indexes.

A71 **VERTICAL FILE INDEX: Subject and Title Index to Selected Pamphlet Material** New York, H.W. Wilson, 1935–
Monthly except August, with annual cumulations. $8/year.
Alphabetical subject listing of free and inexpensive materials
of general interest. Title index follows the subject list.

A72 **WHO WRITES WHAT** Cincinnati and Boston, National
Underwriters Co. 1971. $5.50.
Describes the major types of insurance contracts of life and
health insurance companies.

Textbooks and Consumer Education Materials

In recent years, it has become clear that many consumer problems can be solved only by education and information. The Office of Consumer Affairs, Executive Office of the President, has taken a lead in supporting consumer education programs; universities, secondary, and elementary schools are now including consumer education in their curricula. In addition, many other government and private organizations are supporting consumer education at the adult level, often for low-income groups. Special efforts are also being made to reach foreign-language-speaking immigrants, whose consumer problems are often complicated because of language difficulties.

The items discussed in Directory B consist primarily of textbooks and audiovisual materials which cover both specific aspects of consumer education (e.g., life insurance) and more general information. Additional materials are referenced in the *Consumer Education Bibliography* (see A18) prepared by the Yonkers Public Library for the President's Committee on Consumer Interests.

B1   CONSUMER AND COMMERCIAL CREDIT MANAGEMENT   By Robert Hartzell Cole. Homewood, Ill., R.D. Irwin, 1948. $14; text edition, $10.

This text is planned to give an appreciation of the economic and social implications of credit and to explain the types of credit available.

B2   THE CONSUMER AND HIS DOLLARS   By David

Schoenfeld and Arthur A. Matella. Dobbs Ferry, N.Y., Oceana Publ., 1966. $6.

A secondary school, college, and adult-level textbook designed to develop an awareness of, and alertness to, the importance of making wise consumer decisions.

B3   **CONSUMER BUYING FOR BETTER LIVING** By Cleo Fitzsimmons. New York, Wiley, 1961. $9.90.

A college and university text designed to provide assistance in the activities of consumer or household buying. Reviews problems often encountered by consumers.

B4   **CONSUMER ECONOMIC PROBLEMS** By William Harmon Wilson and Elvin S. Eyster. Cincinnati, Southwestern Publ., 1966. $5.96.

A textbook for consumers that deals with the essentials of economic principles and business relations. A supplement entitled *Buying Guides for Consumer Economic Problems* is available.

B5   **CONSUMER ECONOMICS** By Fred Theodore Wilhelms, Ramon P. Heimerl, and Herbert M. Jelley. New York, McGraw-Hill, 1969. $6.56.

This text provides students with an understanding of the economic system and how to get the most from it. Covers the role of the consumer in the economy.

B6   **CONSUMER EDUCATION: CURRICULUM GUIDE FOR OHIO, GRADES K-12** Columbus, Ohio State University, Instructional Materials Laboratory, Trade and Industrial Education, 1970. $2.75.

A curriculum guide for K-6, 7-12, and specialized groups such as the mentally retarded and socio-economically disadvantaged.

B7   **THE CONSUMER IN AMERICAN SOCIETY; PERSONAL AND FAMILY FINANCE** By Archie William Troelstrup. 4th Edition. New York, McGraw-Hill, 1970. $9.95.

A college-level text on consumer movements, progress of government regulations, and problems confronting consumers.

B8   THE CONSUMER IN SOCIETY   By Leonard T. Kreisman. New York, Odyssey Press, 1964. $4.

A textbook that provides information a well-informed consumer should have in order to make intelligent decisions in our modern society.

B9   THE CONSUMER IN THE MARKETPLACE   By Leon Levy, Robert Feldman, and Simpson Sasserath. New York, Pitman Publ., 1970. $7.33.

This is a text to educate the consumer in both buying methods and saving money, and to help him make better choices.

B10   CONSUMER PROBLEMS AND PERSONAL FINANCE By Archie William Troelstrup. New York, McGraw-Hill, 1965. $9.50.

Written for students and others who desire practical aid in making consumer choices and solving special consumer problems.

B11   ECONOMICS FOR CONSUMERS   By Leland James Gordon and Stewart M. Lee. New York, American Book Co., 1967. $8.95.

Deals with economic principles from the consumer point of view. Covers budgeting, cooperative buying, insurance, shelter, investments, and standards for consumers.

B12   FACTS ABOUT MERCHANDISE   By William Boyd Logan and Helen M. Moon. Englewood Cliffs, N.J., Prentice-Hall, 1967. $7.60.

A textbook that provides up-to-date information on products sold in the retail market. Includes a teachers manual, film lists, and bibliographies.

B13   THE FAMILY AS CONSUMERS   By Irene Oppenheim. New York, Macmillan, 1965. $7.25.

A college-level text on consumer economics and family finance. Provides comprehensive and concise information on the problems and potentials of family spending and consumption.

B14 **FAMILY FINANCIAL MANAGEMENT KIT** By John C. Roman and Robert Finch. 2nd Edition. Cincinnati, Southwestern Publ., 1970. $2.36.
A student kit that provides guidelines for areas such as budgeting and check writing.

B15 **FOOD BUYING; Marketing Information for Consumers** By Carlton E. Wright. New York, Macmillan, 1962. $8.95.
A text that provides food and marketing information to consumers.

B16 **HOME BUYER'S GUIDE** By Jack Wren. New York, Barnes and Noble, 1970. $1.75.
A self-teaching book on selecting, financing, and selling a home. Appendixes include buyer's, seller's, and financial checklists and glossaries on building construction and legal terms.

B17 **KNOW YOUR MERCHANDISE** By Isabel Barnum Wingate et al. New York, McGraw-Hill, 1964. $7.50.
A text primarily for retailing students and for classes in consumer buying. Provides information with which to interpret labels, advertisements, and other sources of information about a product.

B18 **LIFE INSURANCE** By Solomon Stephen Huebner and Kenneth Black, Jr. New York, Appleton-Century-Crofts, 1969. $7.95.
A textbook for selling life and health insurance.

B19 **MODERN CONSUMER EDUCATION** New York, Grolier Education Corp. $200.
A comprehensive study program including 40 selections with answer key cards, student study guides and record books, an instructor's manual, 12 audio tapes, and 2 film strips. Topics include: The Big Things You Buy, Smaller Purchases, The Law and Medicine, Ways to Handle Money, and Ways to Shop. Within the major topics are detailed selections such as Best

Food Buys, Food Planning, Managing Your Money, Labels, Advertisements, and Stores.

B20 **THE NEW APPROACH TO CONSUMER EDUCATION**
In: *Proceedings of the First Regional Conference on Consumer Education*, Yonkers, N.Y., 1968. Albany, University of the State of New York, Curriculum Development Center, 1968. Prices vary.

Papers on Federal Government and consumer interests and reports on health, business education, home economics, and continuing education.

B21 **A RESOURCE KIT FOR TEACHING CONSUMER EDUCATION: The Marketplace** Washington, D.C., Changing Times Education Service, 1971. $44.50.

A multimedia teaching kit that includes instructional guides and materials on advertising, fraud, and safeguards for shoppers.

B22 **SELF-CORRECTING PROBLEMS IN PERSONAL FINANCE** By Robert Dolphin, Jr. Boston, Allyn & Bacon, 1970. $2.50.

A college workbook covering budgeting, insurance, purchasing power, and personal income taxes.

B23 **YOU ARE A CONSUMER—OF CLOTHING** By Pauline Bertie Gillette Garrett and Edward J. Metzer. Boston, Ginn, 1967. $2.80.

A text on the consumer's role, getting his money's worth, where and why to buy, and where to get help; continuing education for consumers.

B24 **YOUR FAMILY AND ITS MONEY** By Helen M. Thal and Melinda Holcombe. Boston, Houghton Mifflin, 1968. $5.20.

A high-school text on family finance that includes a list of resource materials.

C

General Interest

The sources in this Directory were selected for their appeal to individual consumers. Many of them serve as case studies of existing problems; others provide practical "how to" and "how to avoid" guidance; and, in most instances, they provide guides to additional sources of information through organizational listings and bibliographies. Many of these sources are also listed in Directories A and B.

An effort has been made to include titles covering governmental and private programs designed to assist the consumer, since it is felt that this information is important in highlighting major and frequent problems and may serve as a guide on how to file complaints. In a few instances, items describing consumers and their major concerns have been included as a means of alerting others to common problems.

The majority of the publications listed cover specific aspects of consumer information, for example, consumer credit and buying a home; but, a number of general guides to buying any product or service also have been included.

C1 **ALL YOUR HOME BUILDING AND REMODELING QUESTIONS ANSWERED** By Stanley Schuler. New York, Macmillan, 1971. $8.95.

Questions and answers on land purchase, financing, planning, contracting (including sample contracts), equipment, utilities, and remodeling.

C2 **THE AMERICAN WAY OF DEATH** By Jessica Mitford. New York, Simon & Schuster, 1963. $4.95.

Concerns the American funeral, undertakers, cemeteries, and costs. Includes a directory of memorial societies and related organizations, information about eye banks and donation of bodies to medical science, and a bibliography.

C3   **ANNUAL PRICE SURVEY: FAMILY BUDGET COSTS**
13th Edition. New York, Community Council of Greater New York, 1970. $2.50.
Contains weekly costs for individuals, retail price lists, and costs for the "Index Family" and "Retired Couple."

C4   **ANSWERS TO YOUR EVERYDAY MONEY QUES-
TIONS** By Lorraine L. Blair. Chicago, Regnery, 1968. $4.95.
A discussion of good money management.

C5   **THE ASSAULT ON CHILDHOOD!** By Ron Goulard. Los Angeles, Sherbourne Press, 1969. $6.50.
Discusses techniques used by promoters and manufacturers who are involved in the promotion of products directed to youngsters.

C6   **THE BARGAIN HUCKSTERS** By Ralph Lee Smith. New York, Crowell, 1962. $3.95.
Discusses bargain and sales advertising and the growing resentment against, and distrust of, business. Describes huckster's tricks and recommends steps for dealing with them.

C7   **THE BILLION $ SWINDLE, FRAUDS AGAINST THE ELDERLY** New York, Fleet Press, 1969. $5.95.
Reviews problems disclosed by Senate investigations and points out likely areas for fraud.

C8   **BLACK MARKET MEDICINE** By Margaret B. Kreig. Englewood Cliffs, N.J., Prentice-Hall, 1967. $5.95.
A report on the illicit prescription drug industry. Based on undercover investigations conducted by the Food and Drug Administration.

C9   THE BOOM IN GOING BUST By George Sullivan. New York, Macmillan, 1968. $5.95.
Provides facts concerning the problem of personal bankruptcy.

C10   BRANDS, GENERICS, PRICES AND QUALITY: The Prescribing Debate After a Decade Washington, D.C., Pharmaceutical Manufacturers Association, 1971. $1.
Traces developments in the controversy over how drugs are prescribed.

C11   BY PRESCRIPTION ONLY By Morton Mintz. Boston, Houghton Mifflin, 1967. $6.95. Revised edition of an earlier book entitled *The Therapeutic Nightmare*, published in paperback by Beacon ($3.95).
A report on the roles of the Food and Drug Administration, the American Medical Association, pharmaceutical manufacturers, and others in connection with the irrational and massive use of prescription drugs that may be worthless, injurious, or even lethal.

C12   CAN YOU BE SURE OF YOUR EXPERTS? A Complete Manual on How to Choose and Use Doctors, Lawyers, Brokers and All the Other Experts in Your Life By Roger A. Golde. New York, Macmillan, 1969. $5.95.
A complete guide on how to deal with doctors, lawyers, and stock brokers, among others.

C13   CHAMPAGNE LIVING ON A BEER BUDGET; How to Buy the Best for Less By Mike and Marilyn Ferguson. New York, Putnam, 1968. $4.95.
A compendium of information to help the consumer save money.

C14   THE CHEMICAL FEAST: THE NADER SUMMER STUDY GROUP REPORT ON THE FOOD AND DRUG ADMINISTRATION New York, Grossman Publ., 1970. $6.95; paperback, $0.95.
A report covering the lack of control over the chemical environment.

C15 CODES OR DATED EDIBLES, 1971 Prospect Heights, Ill., National Consumers Union, 1971. $0.50.

A useful aid to decoding dates and labels on packaged goods and determining the storage life of frozen foods.

C16 COMMODITY YEARBOOK New York, Commodity Research Bureau, 1939– . Annual. $18.95.

Provides extensive commodity information from both public and private sources, including figures on production, supply and distribution, storage, and average prices.

C17 A COMMONSENSE GUIDE TO DOCTORS, HOSPITALS AND MEDICAL CARE By R.H. Blum. New York, Macmillan, 1964. $5.95.

Practical handbook that provides information on such matters as how to select and use a doctor, how to change doctors, and how to select a hospital and medical insurance.

C18 THE CONSUMER Compiled by Gerald Leinwand. New York, Washington Square Press, 1970. $0.75.

Warns the consumer of pitfalls and points the way to better information. Special attention is given to the dilemmas of the urban consumer.

C19 CONSUMER ACTION GUIDE 1973; What to Do and Who to Call When Things Go Wrong By Joseph Rosenbloom. New York, CCM Information Corporation, 1972. $1.95.

This *Guide* lists more than 7,500 products and services. Manufacturers and suppliers are identified by name, address, and person to contact. Also contains a listing of federal, state, and local agencies.

C20 CONSUMER BEWARE! YOUR FOOD AND WHAT'S BEEN DONE TO IT By Beatrice Trum Hunter. New York, Simon and Schuster, 1971. $8.95.

Describes the effects of what we eat on our health and suggests ways to reverse the present unhealthy trend.

C21 CONSUMER CHOICE IN THE AMERICAN ECONOMY
By Carolyn Shaw Bell. New York, Random House, 1967. $9.50.
Concentrates primarily on consumer behavior, but Chapter 9 is concerned with consumer protection, information for the consumer, and consumer credit.

C22 CONSUMER CREDIT AND THE LOW INCOME CONSUMER Washington, D.C., Urban Coalition, 1969. Free.
A study of efforts to provide information on the availability of credit, counseling, and education to low-income consumers. Covers commercial banks, credit unions, and retailers.

C23 THE CONSUMER IN OUR ECONOMY By David Boyce Hamilton. Boston, Houghton Mifflin, 1962. $8.75.
Primarily devoted to consumer behavior, but includes chapters on consumer aids and their uses; consumer movements; and federal, state, and local governments and the consumer.

C24 CONSUMERISM: A NEW AND GROWING FORCE IN THE MARKETPLACE Washington, D.C., Burson-Marsteller, 1970. Free.
Discusses the consumer movement, federal and state governmental actions, and private organizations; reviews consumer legislation; and recommends industry attitudes toward consumer problems. Also includes "Consumer Laws Now in Effect," "Personalities in the Consumer Movement," "Major Federal Government Agencies with Consumer-Related Responsibilities," "Consumer Product Testing Organizations," and "Private Consumer Organizations."

C25 CONSUMERISM: SEARCH FOR THE CONSUMER INTEREST Compiled by David A. Aaker. New York, Free Press, 1971. $8.95; paperback, $3.95.
A collection of papers on consumerism directed primarily to managers and students of business.

C26 CONSUMER PROPOSALS FOR CLASS ACTIONS AND

OTHER REMEDIES Washington, D.C., American Enterprise Institute for Public Policy Research, 1970. $2.

Covers consumer protection proposals by the 91st Congress, 2nd session.

C27 **CONSUMER PROTECTION AGENCIES: A SURVEY** By John D. Hinkle and Robert P. Nevins. Frankfort, Ky., Legislative Research Commission, 1969. Informational Bulletin No. 79. Free.

A study by the Legislative Research Commission to determine the best—and proper—procedures for establishing and operating a consumer protection agency at the state level.

C28 **CONSUMER PROTECTION IN THE STATES** Lexington, Ky., Council of State Governments, 1970. $3.

Identifies consumer problems and discusses laws that affect consumer affairs.

C29 **CONSUMER PROTECTION PROGRAMS: COMPARATIVE ANALYSIS** By Ronald Sanford. Honolulu, Hawaii University, Economic Research Center, 1962. $1.

A comparison of consumer programs, consumer representation in government, federal concern with consumer protection, and state consumer protection programs in New York, Massachusetts, and California. Covers the role of the Better Business Bureaus in affording consumer protection.

C30 **CONSUMER'S BUYING GUIDE: How to Get Your Money's Worth** Association of Better Business Bureaus. New York, Benjamin Company, 1968. $1.

Discusses Better Business Bureaus, consumers and consumer reports, places to live, automobiles, food, and clothing.

C31 **THE CONSUMER'S GUIDE TO BETTER BUYING** By Sidney Margolius. Rev. ed. New York, Pocket Books, 1972. $1.25.

This is a revised edition of an earlier, practical guide on how to find the best values in products, food, insurance, and hundreds of other items.

C32 **THE CONSUMER'S GUIDE TO INSURANCE BUYING** By Vladimir P. Chernik. Los Angeles, Sherbourne Press, 1970. $6.50.

A guide to buying insurance. Discusses each type, the problems with each, and best buys.

C33 **THE CONSUMER'S HANDBOOK; 100 WAYS TO GET MORE VALUE FOR YOUR DOLLARS** By the Editors of the National Observer. Princeton, N.J., Dow Jones Books, 1969. $1.85.

Points out the need for a continuous flow of information on available products and services. Material is compiled from weekly *National Observer* articles and news accounts for the shopper.

C34 **CONSUMER SWINDLERS, AND HOW TO AVOID THEM** By John L. Springer. Chicago, Regnery, 1970. $5.95.

How to avoid swindles by repairmen when making home improvements, when buying land, and in other areas.

C35 **THE CONSUMING PUBLIC** Edited by Grant S. McClellan. Bronx, N.Y., H.W. Wilson, 1968. $3.50.

A compilation of articles, papers, and speeches concerned with consumer problems and consumer protection.

C36 **CRC HANDBOOK OF FOOD ADDITIVES** Edited by Thomas E. Furia. Cleveland, Chemical Rubber Co., 1968. $22.50.

Provides information on the properties and uses of direct food ingredients and food additives.

C37 **CREDIT JUNGLE** By Al Griffin. Chicago, Regnery, 1971. $5.95.

Deals with credit cards, revolving charge accounts, and installment plans, especially the credit practices used with low-income groups.

C38 **CRISIS IN CAR INSURANCE** Edited by Robert E. Keeton et al. Urbana, Ill., University of Illinois Press, 1968. $6.95.
Eight papers and a summary report of the proceedings of the national conference on car insurance sponsored by the College of Law (October 1967).

C39 **THE DARK SIDE OF THE MARKETPLACE; The Plight of the American Consumer** By Warren Grant Magnuson and Jean Carper. Englewood Cliffs, N.J., Prentice-Hall, 1968. $5.95.
Presents examples of actual problems faced by consumers.

C40 **DEBTORS' AND CREDITORS': RIGHTS AND REME-DIES** By Sidney Sherwin. Jamaica, N.Y., Attorneys' Aid Publ., 1969. $12.95.
A practical guide to legal rights and remedies of debtors and creditors. Includes 28 legal forms.

C41 **DICTOCRATS** By Omar V. Garrison. New York, Arco, 1971. $1.25.
The author presents his views on existing corruption in federal bureaus, especially the Food and Drug Administration.

C42 **THE DOLLAR SQUEEZE AND HOW TO BEAT IT** By George Sullivan. New York, Macmillan, 1970. $5.95.
Covers credit and debt, buymanship, budgeting, and handling a second income.

C43 **DON'T YOU BELIEVE IT** By Frederick John Schliank and M.C. Phillips. New York, Pyramid Publ., 1966. $0.75.
Advises consumers on how to avoid being taken in by today's flood of false advertising, hidden-cost premium deals, quack cures and remedies, and phoney discount arrangements.

C44 **ECONOMIC ALMANAC** Edited by Paul Biederman, National Industrial Conference Board. New York, Macmillan, 1940– . Biannual. $2.95.

Provides statistical data for such areas as income, agriculture, construction and housing, personal consumption and savings, service, banking, and finance.

C45 THE ECONOMICS OF TRADING STAMPS By Harold W. Fox. Washington, D.C., Public Affairs Press, 1968. $6.

Analyzes the trading-stamp industry—its organization and performance—and covers functions, costs, and benefits of its services.

C46 FAMILY CREDIT COUNSELING—AN EMERGING COMMUNITY SERVICE By Perry B. Hall, Study Director, National Study Service. New York, Family Service Association of America, 1968. $8.75; paperback, $1.50.

A study of family credit counseling provided through non-profit community-based programs.

C47 FEDERAL CONSUMER SAFETY LEGISLATION; A STUDY OF THE SCOPE AND ADEQUACY OF THE AUTOMOBILE SAFETY, FLAMMABLE FABRICS, TOYS AND HAZARDOUS SUBSTANCES PROGRAMS By Howard A. Heffron. Washington, D.C., National Commission on Product Safety, 1970. $1.25.

A special report, prepared for the National Commission on Product Safety, concerned with how three major consumer safety programs have worked: the National Traffic and Motor Vehicle Safety Act, the Flammable Fabrics Act, and the Federal Hazardous Substances Act.

C48 THE FEDERAL TRADE COMMISSION By Susan Wagner. New York, Praeger, 1971. $7.95.

A study of the Federal Trade Commission—its purpose, organization, and methods of operation.

C49 FINANCIAL SELF-DEFENSE By John L. Springer. New York, McGraw-Hill, 1969. $5.95.

A basic guide to personal finance. Covers taxes, credit insurance, gyps and rackets, investments, and inflation.

C50 THE GERBER REPORT: A Doctor's Diagnosis and Prescription By Alex Gerber. New York, David McKay, 1971. $6.95.

Discusses bad medical practices, poor hospital care, and exploitation. Offers some constructive suggestions on eliminating bad medical practices.

C51 GETTING THE MOST FOR YOUR MONEY; How to Beat the High Cost of Living By Anthony Scaduto. New York, David McKay, 1970. $6.95.

A down-to-earth discussion of the problems facing consumers in such areas as gimmick advertising and contracts. Chapter 2, "Where to Get Help," is intended for the individual consumer, but it also provides a source list for libraries, information centers, and organized groups.

C52 THE GHETTO MARKETPLACE Edited by Frederick D. Sturdivant. New York, Free Press, 1969. $7.95; paperback, $3.95.

A collection of articles and other materials on the problems confronting the urban poor in the marketplace.

C53 THE GREAT AMERICAN FOOD HOAX By Sidney Margolius. New York, Walker, 1971. $5.95.

Discusses the rising cost of food and the decline of the nutrition level.

C54 THE GREAT VITAMIN HOAX By Daniel Takton. New York, Macmillan, 1968. $5.95.

Presentation of vitamin hucksters as the author sees them.

C55 HANDBOOK ON CONSUMER LAW National Institute for Education in Law and Poverty. Evanston, Ill., Northwestern University School of Law, 1968. $10.

A guide to assist the legal service attorney in his representation of the poor.

C56 HANDLING YOUR MONEY By Anthony Scaduto. New York, David McKay, 1970. $6.95.

Contains advice on consolidating loans, housing, credit, taxes, and investments.

C57 HEALTH: A CONSUMER'S DILEMMA By Robert E. Kime. Belmont, Calif., Wadsworth Publ., 1970. $1.25.

A guide to aid the consumer in making health-care decisions.

C58 HEARING AIDS Edited by L.R. Corliss, National Bureau of Standards. Washington, D.C., U.S. Government Printing Office, 1970. Number SP C13.14:117. $0.35.

Provides consumer guidance in the selection and care of hearing aids.

C59 THE HIDDEN ASSASSINS By Booth Mooney. Chicago, Follett Publ., 1966. $4.95.

Discusses food additives, food quackery, and other food-related problems, including a chapter on what can be done to remedy these problems.

C60 THE HOMEOWNER'S SURVIVAL KIT By Arthur Martin Watkins. New York, Hawthorne, 1971. $6.95.

Deals with general household costs and how they can be reduced. Among the subjects covered are monthly costs for utilities, telephone, home repairs, heating, air conditioning, and property insurance.

C61 HOT WAR ON THE CONSUMER By David Sanford et al. New York, Pitman Publ., 1969. $5.95.

A collection of articles—primarily from the *New Republic*— on food and drugs, big business malpractice, safety, and insurance.

C62 THE HOUSE YOU WANT: HOW TO FIND IT—HOW TO BUY IT By Lila Perl. Pleasantville, N.Y., Funk & Wagnalls, 1965. $1.50.

Buying, building, and selling a house are discussed in detail.

C63 HOW TO AVOID A REAL ESTATE AGENT By Ruth Mayer and Lucille Bowman. New York, Morrow, 1969. $4.95; paperback, $2.45.

Describes the step-by-step details involved in buying and selling a house without an agent, such as arriving at realistic prices, when and where to advertise, information to have available for the buyers, and cleaning and preparing the house and grounds.

C64 HOW TO BUY A HOME—HOW TO SELL A HOME By Glenn Fowler. New York, Rutledge Books, 1969. $1.45.

A comprehensive guide for buying and selling a home. Includes a checklist to use when buying.

C65 HOW TO BUY A HOUSE By Byron Moger and Martin Burke. New York, Lyle Stuart, 1969. $4.95.

Contains answers to most questions on buying a house.

C66 HOW TO BUY THE RIGHT HOUSE AT THE RIGHT PRICE By Robert W. Murray, Jr. New York, Macmillan, 1965. $0.95.

Comprehensive coverage on locating a house and the closing and financing procedures involved when buying a house.

C67 HOW TO GET OUT OF DEBT—AND STAY OUT OF DEBT By Merle E. Dowd. Chicago, Regnery, 1971. $5.95.

A discussion of economical food preparation, how to cut down on clothing expenses, ways one can find free entertainment, and methods of solving problems associated with too large a debt.

C68 HOW TO LIVE ON YOUR INCOME Edited by *Reader's Digest* Staff. New York, Norton, 1970. $8.95.

Covers personal finance, with a section on the provisions of income tax reform.

C69 HOW TO MAKE THE MOST OF YOUR MONEY By

Sidney Margolius. New York, Meredith Press, 1969. $6.95; paperback, $3.95.

Discusses housing costs, unexpected medical bills, car and transportation expenses, and college costs.

C70 **HOW TO REDUCE YOUR MEDICAL BILLS** By Ruth Winter. New York, Crown, 1970. $5.95.

Deals with the problems of medical costs and presents some already effective and proposed solutions. Each chapter ends with an annotated list of suggestions on how to obtain effective health care. Contains a list of health-related societies and organizations, statistical tables on medical personnel, a list of physician-assistant training programs, and names and addresses of many community health centers.

C71 **HOW TO SHAKE THE MONEY TREE** By Robert Metz. New York, Putnam, 1966. $5.95.

Provides information on credit, low-cost money sources, when to pay the piper, special-purpose loans and grants, small loans, the Small Business Administration, and where to borrow money for business purposes.

C72 **HOW TO TALK BACK TO YOUR TELEVISION SET** By Nicholas Johnson. Boston, Little Brown, 1970. $0.95.

How to complain and effectively petition to improve TV programming. Lists free material and local information available.

C73 **HOW YOU CAN BEAT INFLATION** By David L. Markstein. New York, McGraw-Hill, 1970. $7.95.

Provides specific information on food, shelter, services, and investments.

C74 **THE INNOCENT CONSUMER VS. THE EXPLOITERS** By Sidney Margolius. New York, Trident Press, 1967. $4.95.

A discussion of consumer exploitation, with a guide to sources for assistance. Appendix A contains a list of National Consumer Organizations and County and City Organizations. Appendix B is a listing of Better Business Bureaus.

C75 THE INNOCENT INVESTOR AND THE SHAKY GROUND FLOOR By Sidney Margolius. New York, Trident Press, 1971. $6.95.

A discussion of how to protect oneself against hard-sell promoters and big institutions that nibble at investment earnings.

C76 LEGAL PROTECTION FOR THE CONSUMER By Paul Crown. Dobbs Ferry, N.Y., Oceana Publ., 1963. $3.

A guide to the various types of legal protection available to the consumer.

C77 MANAGING YOUR FAMILY FINANCES J. K. Lasser Tax Institute. New York, Doubleday, 1968. $5.95.

Provides guidance for effective money management.

C78 MANUAL OF SIMPLE BURIAL Edited by Ernest Morgan. Burnsville, N.C., Celo Press, 1965. $1.

Discusses memorial, funeral, and burial societies and includes a list of these societies located in the United States and Canada.

C79 THE MEDICAL MESSIAHS By James Harvey Young. Princeton, N.J., Princeton University Press, 1967. $9.

Comprehensive treatment of the concurrent rise in 20th Century America of modern medical science and pseudomedical nonsense. Trends in quackery are studied in the broader sense of self-medication.

C80 THE MEDICAL OFFENDERS By Howard R. and Martha Lewis. New York, Simon & Schuster, 1970. $7.50.

Reveals the problems faced by consumers concerning medical services.

C81 THE MORTALITY MERCHANTS: The Legalized Racket of Life Insurance and What You Can Do About It By G. Scott Reynolds. New York, David McKay, 1968. $5.95.

Describes life insurance companies and the policies they offer.

C82 THE MOST FOR THEIR MONEY: A REPORT Washington, D.C., United States Panel on Consumer Education for Persons with Limited Incomes, 1965. Free.

Deals with special problems of the poor in the marketplace—including lack of knowledge and information—with a discussion of the role that consumer education can play in solving these problems. Appendix I includes a list of resources for consumer education; Appendix II lists headquarters' addresses of federal departments and agencies; Appendix III lists federal grants and financial assistance programs available for consumer education; and Appendix IV lists members of the Panel.

C83 MOVING: A COMMONSENSE GUIDE TO RELOCAT-ING YOUR FAMILY By Edith Ruina. Pleasantville, N.Y., Funk & Wagnalls, 1970. $8.95.

Provides information on selling a home, packing and moving schedules, relocating, making legal and financial arrangements, and adjusting to the new environment.

C84 OVERCHARGE By Lee Metcalf and Vic Reinemer. New York, David McKay, 1967. $5.95.

Advises the consumer of what he can do about exploitation by electric utility companies.

C85 THE PLOT TO MAKE YOU BUY By John Fisher. New York, McGraw-Hill, 1968. $2.95.

Examines the effects of marketing practices on consumers—especially programs of planned obsolescence—and appeals for controls on the enormous amounts of money and power wielded by organized marketing interests.

C86 POISONS IN YOUR FOOD By Ruth Winter. New York, Crown Publ., 1969. $5.95.

A compendium of information on health hazards in food.

C87 THE POOR PAY MORE; CONSUMER PRACTICES OF LOW-INCOME FAMILIES By David Caplovitz. New York, Free Press, 1967. $2.45.

As a result of an in-depth study of the buying power of low-income families in three New York settlements, a consumer education program is provided that gives insights into types of problems to avoid.

C88 **A PRIMER ON THE LAW OF DECEPTIVE PRACTICES** By Earl W. Kintner. New York, Macmillan, 1971. $12.95.
Provides an introduction to existing legislation that regulates the conduct of business.

C89 **THE RADICAL CONSUMER'S HANDBOOK** By Goody L. Solomon. New York, Ballantine, 1972. $1.25.
A guide to consumers' rights in the marketplace. Stresses the importance of knowledge regarding these rights.

C90 **THE REGULATORS: WATCHDOG AGENCIES AND THE PUBLIC INTEREST** By Louis M. Kohlmeier, Jr. New York, Harper & Row, 1969. $8.95.
Points out how the federal regulatory agencies have failed to protect the consumer.

C91 **REPORT OF THE TASK FORCE ON APPLIANCE WARRANTIES AND SERVICE** Washington, D.C., Department of Commerce, 1969. Free.
Prepared jointly by the Departments of Labor and Commerce, the Federal Trade Commission, and the Special Assistant to the President for Consumer Affairs. Includes problems, product performance, product information, recommendations, and a summary of state regulations.

C92 **THE RIGHT TO LIVE** By Ronald D. Damerow. New York, Vantage, 1971. $4.95.
Discusses the drug trade, pharmaceutical research, and the Food and Drug Administration.

C93 **SAVE YOUR HEALTH AND YOUR MONEY: A DOCTOR'S ANSWERS TO TODAY'S HIGH HEALTH COSTS** By Patrick J. Doyle. New York, Acropolis, 1971. $6.95.

Provides information on how to select and evaluate physicians, dentists, hospitals, and insurance policies; how to keep drug costs down; and where to obtain free medical information and services.

C94   SMART SHOPPER'S GUIDE   By Aileen Snoddy. New York, Arco Publ., 1965. $2.50; paperback, $1.00.
A buyer's guide for major purchases that sets forth such facts as specific design, performance, and engineering to assist the consumer in comparing items being purchased. Includes questions one should ask before buying.

C95   SOWING THE WIND: The Nader Summer Study Group Report on Food, Pesticides, and the Poor as Affected by the Department of Agriculture   Edited by Harrison Wellford. New York, Grossman Publ., 1970. $7.95; paperback, $0.95.
A critical discussion of the Department of Agriculture and its operations.

C96   SO YOU WANT TO BUY A MOBILE HOME   By Al Griffin. Chicago, Regnery, 1970. $5.95.
Information is given on design, construction, dealers, sites for locating mobile homes, and financing. Contains a list of mobile home manufacturers, with the types of units built by each.

C97   STATISTICAL ABSTRACT OF THE UNITED STATES   U.S. Bureau of the Census. Washington, D.C., U.S. Government Printing Office, 1878– . Annual. $5.50.
Includes statistics on consumer cooperatives, the cost of living, credit, and price indexes.

C98   THE SUPERMARKET TRAP: THE CONSUMER AND THE FOOD INDUSTRY   By Jennifer Cross. Bloomington, Ind., Indiana University Press, 1970. $6.95.
A survey of food industry operations.

C99   THE THUMB ON THE SCALE OR, THE SUPERMARKET SHELL GAME   By A.Q. Mowbray. Philadelphia, Lippincott, 1967. $4.95.

Author's view of packaging abuses and business pressures by supermarkets.

C100 **THE TIME-LIFE BOOK OF FAMILY FINANCE** By Carlton Smith et al. Boston, Little, Brown, 1969. $11.95.
Provides numerous charts and graphs related to family finances.

C101 **TOP SHOPS & SECRET SERVICES, WASHINGTON, D.C. AREA** By Betty Mintz. Washington, D.C., Plymouth Printing, 1970. $2.50.
A guide to shopping in Washington, D.C., with emphasis on quality and price. The first section includes listings of both emergency and general information services, with telephone numbers. The second section is devoted to shops and restaurants.

C102 **TOYS THAT DON'T CARE** By Edward M. Swartz. Boston, Gambit, 1971. $6.95.
Warns the consumer about injuries children can receive from toys.

C103 **A TREATISE ON THE LAW OF FOODS, DRUGS AND COSMETICS** By Harry Toulmin. Cincinnati, W.H. Anderson Co., 1963. $110.
Provides information about laws, their purposes and legislative history, and court rulings as they pertain to foods, drugs, and cosmetics.

C104 **TRENDS IN CONSUMER CREDIT LEGISLATION** By Barbara A. Curran. Chicago, University of Chicago Press, 1965. $8.50.
Surveys the relevant statutory materials on consumer credit.

C105 **THE TROUBLE WITH LAWYERS** By Murray Teigh Bloom. New York, Simon & Schuster, 1969. $1.25.
Describes the problems faced by middle-class Americans when they require legal services.

C106 TRUTH IN ADVERTISING AND OTHER HERESIES
By Walter Weir. New York, McGraw-Hill, 1963. $6.50.
Acknowledges criticisms leveled at advertising and indicates steps which could be taken to correct abuses.

C107 TWO HUNDRED TRICKS TO BEAT INFLATION New York, Dell, 1970. $0.25.
Provides the housewife with helpful hints on how to save money when buying for the family.

C108 UNFIT FOR HUMAN CONSUMPTION By Ruth Mulvey Harmer. Englewood Cliffs, N.J., Prentice-Hall, 1971. $6.95.
Discusses the dangers of food contamination through unrestricted use of pesticides.

C109 USING OUR CREDIT INTELLIGENTLY Washington, D.C., National Foundation for Consumer Credit, 1968. Free.
A discussion of consumer credit, forms of credit, creating a budget, and using credit.

C110 THE VULNERABLE AMERICANS By Curt Gentry. Garden City, N.Y., Doubleday, 1966. $4.95.
Fraud in insurance, credit cards, health and medicine, and repairs is discussed.

C111 THE WASTE MAKERS By Vance Packard. New York, David McKay, 1960. $6.50.
Author describes how quickly consumer products wear out; deplores the lack of widespread concern about the efficiency and durability of products consumers buy.

C112 WEIGHTS AND MEASURES AND THE CONSUMER By Leland J. Gordon. New York, Consumers Union, 1970. $3.
A discussion of what consumers need to know about weights and measures. A survey of state legislation, administration, and enforcement activities is included.

C113 WHAT TO DO WITH YOUR BAD CAR: An Action Man-

ual for Lemon Owners By Ralph Nader et al. New York, Grossman Publ., 1971. $8.95; paperback, $2.95.

Tells how to reduce your chances of buying a defective car and what to do if you have one.

C114 **WHAT YOU SHOULD KNOW BEFORE YOU HAVE YOUR CAR REPAIRED** By Anthony Till. Los Angeles, Sherbourne Press, 1970. $0.60.

Information on how to protect oneself against bad practices in the auto repair business. Includes a *Flat-Rate Book* that shows what major and minor repair jobs should cost.

C115 **THE WOLVES, WIDOWS AND ORPHANS** By Dan Tyler Moore. Cleveland, World Publ., 1967. $5.95.

Provides case studies of frauds. The last chapter gives rules for protecting oneself against confidence men.

C116 **YOUR PERSONAL GUIDE TO SUCCESSFUL RETIREMENT** By Sidney Margolius. New York, Random House, 1969. $6.95; paperback, $3.95.

Offers comprehensive advice on planning for retirement.

Periodicals

There are three groups of periodicals that can be sources of consumer information:

◇ *Consumer Journals* These periodicals are oriented specifically to news about consumer activities. Many of the organizations listed in Part II of this *Guide* publish such journals.

◇ *Trade Papers and Magazines* These publications are intended for specific industries and businesses. They present the views of the manufacturer, wholesaler, and retailer on issues of interest to the consumer.

◇ *General-Interest and Women's Magazines* Most of these publish articles that are pertinent to consumer affairs.

This Directory lists 65 such periodicals.

CONSUMER JOURNALS

D1 **THE ACCI NEWSLETTER** American Council on Consumer Interests, 238 Stanley Hall, University of Missouri, Columbia, Mo. 65201. 9 issues/year. $6/year.

　　The *Newsletter* includes up-to-date information on new consumer legislation, programs, and activities, as well as announcements of new consumer education materials.

D2 **CHANGING TIMES** Kiplinger Washington Editors, Inc., 1729 H St., N.W., Washington, D.C. 20006. Monthly. $7/year.

Presents short articles on everyday problems in education, medicine, science, religion, and the arts, as well as taxes, advertising, insurance, real estate, interest rates, investments, and which products to buy. Simple graphs, charts, and statistics clarify the more difficult topics. Special features include "Your Questions Answered," "Things to Write For," "Paperback Bookshelf," and "What Uncle Sam Buys." "Got a Gripe? Here's Where to Complain" in the March 1970 issue gives names and addresses of 111 groups offering consumer assistance. Sample pages from this journal are shown in Figures 1 and 2.

They promise action on consumer complaints

Names, addresses, phone numbers of company and government people whose job is to help consumers.

YOU BUY AN APPLIANCE, a car or some other product and it doesn't live up to expectations. You grouse to the salesman or complain to the manager. Nothing happens. Where can you turn? Who will listen to your problem?

Until recently there was not much outlet for consumer frustration. But now unhappy buyers are more vocal, and firms that value their customers are beginning to take notice. Company after company has set up a "department of con-

sumer affairs," a "consumer advocate" or a corporate "ombudsman" to deal with customer complaints. The federal government also has number of consumer affairs offices where embittered buyers can take their grievances.

What do these consumer affairs people do? Most of them say their job is to receive complaints and run down the trouble so that wrong can be put to right. The letters and calls they get also help them pinpoint problem areas that

18   **CHANGING TIMES** *The Kiplinger Magazine*   *January 1972*

Figure 1. This article in Changing Times *lists groups that will help consumers.*

they try to clear up to prevent future trouble.

Are they effective? Yes and no. Some companies do a good job of trying to get at a problem and solve it, others talk a lot about their concern for the customer but they don't do much. Still, the point remains that business and government are awake to the fact that consumers these days are knowledgeable and won't put up with shoddy treatment.

To find out just where a consumer should complain, *Changing Times* queried a number of corporations and government agencies. On the next two pages are the addresses of offices to call or write to if you have a gripe (area code 800 is toll-free). It's not a comprehensive list, but it does indicate the growing number of businesses that at least say they are trying to do something about complaints.

Before you fire off a salvo about the difficulties you're having with a product, here are some suggestions to help you cope with the problem:
► Read the instruction manual, the hang tags or any care instructions to make sure that you have followed directions.
► Know the provisions of your warranty.
► When you register a complaint, present all the facts in the case. Supply your name, ad-

dress, phone number, and make, model and serial number of the car, appliance or product. Give the name and address of the store or dealer and the date the article was purchased. Describe clearly and completely the nature of the problem. Keep a dated copy or record of any complaints.
► If you cannot resolve the problem locally, contact the manufacturer.
► As a court of last resort on major appliances —home laundry equipment, ranges, refrigerators, disposers—get in touch with MACAP (Major Appliance Consumer Action Panel), 20 N. Wacker Dr., Chicago, Ill. 60606. Call collect: (312) 236-3165.

What happened?

Have you made a complaint to any of the consumer-service officers listed on the next two pages? Or to similar officials in other companies or government agencies? If so, what was your experience? What kind of results did you get? Please write us a brief account of how you fared.

Where to complain

AMERICAN MOTORS
Owner Relations Dept.
American Motors Corp.
14250 Plymouth Rd.
Detroit, Mich. 48232
(313) 493-2341

AVIS
Mr. Kenneth N. Safon
Customer Service Manager
Avis Rent-A-Car System, Inc.
900 Old Country Rd.
Garden City, N.Y. 11530
(800) 231-6000
Tex. residents: (800) 392-3966
Mechanical problems and customer travel information

CHASE MANHATTAN
Miss Marjorie P. Meares
Consumer Affairs Officer
Chase Manhattan Bank
One Chase Manhattan Plaza
New York, N.Y. 10015
(212) 552-6343

CHRYSLER
"My Man in Detroit"
Chrysler Corp.
P.O. Box 1086
Detroit, Mich. 48231
The "Man in Detroit" staff directs communications to one of nearly 60 executives responsible for action in various departments. On parts or service problems, the executive telephones the regional office nearest the customer and this office deals with the problem.

CONTINENTAL BAKING
Mr. Paul Khan, Director of
Food Protection
ITT Continental Baking Co.
P.O. Box 731
~stead Ave

Rye, N.Y. 10580
(914) 967-4747, ext. 474

FIRESTONE
Mr. Jack B. Scarcliff
Director of Consumer Affairs
Firestone Tire and Rubber Co.
1200 Firestone Pkwy.
Akron, Ohio 44317
(216) 379-7085

FORD
"We Listen Better"
P.O. Box 1958
The American Rd.
Dearborn, Mich. 48121
Ford has a heavily staffed Customer Service Division. Calls or letters to division headquarters in Dearborn are referred to district offices.

GENERAL ELECTRIC
Evelyn Reynolds
Consumer Affairs
General Electric Co.
Rm. 801
570 Lexington Ave.
New York, N.Y. 10022

GENERAL MILLS
Consumer Coordinator
General Mills, Inc.
9200 Wayzata Blvd.
Minneapolis, Minn. 55440
For information about the company's products or home-making services, write to Mercedes A. Bates, Vice-President and Director of the Betty Crocker Kitchens at the address above.

GENERAL MOTORS
Mr. G.W. Warren, Manager
Owner Relations
General Motors Corp.
General Motors Bldg.
3044 W. Grand Blvd.
Detroit, Mich. 48282
Problems not resolved by dealers are handled ' the zone ~ntral offic~· '   ~er

relations department for each car division and GMC truck and coach division. These addresses are given in owner's manuals.
For Frigidaire products:
Frigidaire Division
Customer Relations Dept.
300 Taylor St.
Dayton, Ohio 45401
(513) 445-5000

GIANT FOOD
Mrs. Esther Peterson
Consumer Advisor
Giant Food, Inc.
Box 1804
Washington, D.C. 20013

GRAND UNION
Miss Jean F. Judge
Director of Consumer Affairs
Grand Union Co.
East Paterson, N.J. 07407

HONEYWELL
Mr. Joseph G. Brodnicki
Director of Consumer Affairs
Honeywell, Inc.
2701 Fourth Ave. S.
Minneapolis, Minn. 55408

HUMBLE
Dr. John B. Boatwright
Consumer Affairs Coordinator
Humble Oil & Refining Co.
Marketing Dept.
P.O. Box 2180
Houston, Tex. 77001

JEWEL FOOD STORES
Mr. Richard Larson
Manager, Customer Relations
Jewel Food Stores
1955 W. North Ave.
Melrose Park, Ill. 60160

MORTON FROZEN FOODS
Mr. Ben A. Murray
Director of Quality Control
Morton Frozen Foods
P ~ Box 731
` Ave.

Rye, N.Y. 10580
(914) 967-4747
Ask for "Virginia Morton"

MOTOROLA
Mr. George Dattilo
Consumer Relations Manager
Motorola, Inc.
Consumer Products Div.
9401 W. Grand Ave.
Franklin Park, Ill. 60131

PAN AMERICAN
Mr. John M. Barnes
Staff Vice-President
Office of Consumer Action
Pan American World
Airways, Inc.
Pan Am Bldg.
New York, N.Y. 10017
(212) 973-4674

RCA
Mr. Herbert T. Brunn
Vice-President, Consumer
Affairs
RCA Corp.
30 Rockefeller Plaza
New York, N.Y. 10020
Covers customer relations in RCA's divisions and subsidiaries, which include Hertz Corp., Banquet Foods, Random House, Coronet Industries (floor coverings, furniture) RCA Global Communications, RCA Records, RCA ServiceCo. and RCA Consumer Electronic products.

SHERATON HOTELS
Miss Barbara J. Mellin
Manager, Guest Relations
ITT Sheraton Corp. of America
470 Atlantic Ave.
Boston, Mass. 02210
(617) 482-1250

TAPPAN
Mr. David C. Rainey
Director of Consumer Relations
Tappan Co.
250 W   e St.
M   ^io 44902

Figure 1. Cont'd

The FTC gets tough

Critics said it wasn't doing enough to protect consumers.
Now it's trying to, but the obstacles are
many and the going is slow.

IT'S REALLY IRONIC. A few years ago consumer advocates were saying the Federal Trade Commission wasn't doing its job of protecting innocent consumers from unfair or deceptive business practices.

Today the chairman of the commission has to defend the agency against business advocates who say that innocent companies are being sacrificed to consumerism.

This new criticism at least indicates the changes that have taken place at the FTC recently. To the companies it regulates, the FTC looks a lot tougher.

New people, new approaches

THE CHANGES began to appear in 1969 after an American Bar Association panel studied the comatose agency at the request of President Nixon. The group confirmed reports by critics (notably Ralph Nader's "raiders") and recommended some strong medicine for revitalizing it. The agency perked up under Caspar Weinberger, who was named chairman in 1970, and the work he started has been continued by the current chairman, Miles Kirkpatrick, who headed the ABA study group.

Operating bureaus were cut from four to two —the Bureau of Competition, which handles

antitrust cases, and the Bureau of Consumer Protection, headed by Robert Pitofsky, who was counsel for the ABA panel. He is only one of many zealous staff people brought in to help revitalize the agency. Others work under him as heads of divisions involved with consumer credit, national advertising and industry rules and guides.

The commission also created a new type of staff position, the consumer-protection specialist, and sent over 100 of these "paralegal" specialists to work in teams with attorneys in the FTC's 11 regional offices. They do investigative work previously handled by attorneys, check business practices, and maintain contact with other consumer enforcement agencies and consumer groups.

Stronger regional offices. The revamping extends to the regional offices, which were given new authority to investigate problems in their areas, hold public hearings and argue their own cases before FTC hearing examiners.

In the past year or so, for example, the Cleveland and New York regional offices have held hearings on consumer problems of poor people, deceptive practices by auto dealers and unfair credit collection practices.

As a result of strengthening the regional of-

Figure 2. The work of the FTC to protect consumers is described in this article from Changing Times.

fices, action probably will be taken against individual companies by the FTC as well as by state and local agencies; some states are moving to tighten their laws; and the FTC staff in Washington is studying recommendations for broader action against certain practices.

A number of regional offices have set up consumer-protection coordinating committees to help federal, state and local consumer-protection offices in an area work more effectively.

In San Francisco, for instance, 13 enforcement agencies use a joint post office number (P.O. Box 700) that bay area residents can send complaints to. The FTC regional office supplies the committee with a full-time staff person to work with volunteer law students in sifting the complaints and then sending them to the proper agency. In cases where agency jurisdictions overlap, the committee might decide to let the office with the strongest remedies take action first, with the rest providing back-up support.

The complaints are computer-tabulated by type of problem. Periodic checks help detect trends in deception, which can then be solved by more action, greater consumer education and, in some cases, better legislation.

Bay area residents can also check the telephone directory under "consumer complaints" for a listing by type of problem. Thus, if a person has been bilked by an auto-repair outfit, he can get the number of the agency that can best handle the complaint.

Tougher enforcement. The real change, though, is how the FTC now polices the marketplace. In the past it had been accused of letting companies off too easy after they had made a lot of money deceiving people. Some recent cases show that the agency can be tough.

► *Give the money back.* Several California mortgage brokers, under a consent order, will have to repay loan service charges the companies didn't disclose as required under the federal truth-in-lending law. The companies—Union Mortgage, Hacienda Home Loans and Stockton Home Mortgage—also agreed to obey federal laws that demand inclusion of the cost of loan service and of credit life and other insurance in the finance charge and to tell borrowers the correct annual percentage rate of loans.

The FTC issued a proposed complaint against Koscot Interplanetary, Inc., a cosmetic marketing firm, whose alleged pyramid-selling arrangement the FTC says may be illegal. The commission said it might ask the company to repay people who lost money investing in the scheme.

► *Fill orders promptly.* Two mail-order outfits —World Art Group and Standard American Suppliers—agreed to give full refunds if they can't ship prepaid orders within 21 days.

► *Stop dangerous practices.* The FTC has limited authority to impose bans by injunction but has moved when it could in several cases. For instance, the agency, concerned about the danger to children, planned to get a court injunction to stop a division of Philip Morris from sending sample razor blades into millions of homes via supplements in Sunday newspapers. Under the threat of a ban, the company voluntarily scotched the plan.

If you've been bilked ...

The Federal Trade Commission can't act on behalf of an individual consumer. And at present, with few exceptions, it can only act against firms that do business in more than one state (Congress is considering a law that would give it wider powers).

However, your complaint along with others could make the commission decide to act against a company to get it to discontinue deceptive practices.

You can send complaints to the FTC Regional Office in your area. The asterisk denotes those offices that have consumer protection coordinating committees, so if your problem can't be handled by the commission it will be sent to the proper federal, state or local protection agency.

730 Peachtree St., N.E.
Atlanta, Ga. 30308

John F. Kennedy Federal Bldg.
Government Center
*Boston, Mass. 02203

Everett McKinley Dirksen Bldg.
219 S. Dearborn St.
*Chicago, Ill. 60604

Federal Office Bldg.
1240 E. Ninth St.
*Cleveland, Ohio 44199
(Coordinating committee at field station:
333 Mt. Elliot Ave.
Detroit, Mich. 48207)

Federal Office Bldg.
911 Walnut St.
Kansas City, Mo. 64106

Federal Bldg.
11000 Wilshire Blvd.
*Los Angeles, Cal. 90024

Masonic Temple Bldg.
333 St. Charles St.
New Orleans, La. 70130

Federal Bldg.
26 Federal Plaza
*New York, N.Y. 10007

Box 36005
450 Golden Gate Ave.
*San Francisco, Cal. 94102

Republic Bldg.
1511 Third Ave.
Seattle, Wash. 98101

2120 L St., N.W.
*Washington, D.C. 20037
(Coordinating committee at field station:
1406 Bankers Security Bldg.
1315 Walnut St.
Philadelphia, Pa. 19107)

Figure 2. Cont'd

D3 **CONSUMER ALERT** Federal Trade Commission, Washington, D.C. 20580. Monthly. Free.
A monthly review of FTC activities.

D4 **CONSUMER BULLETIN** Consumers' Research, Inc., Washington, N.J. 07882. Monthly. $8/year, including *Annual*.
The *Bulletin* presents ratings of products by brand name. On the basis of product testing or examination, a product or service is given a rating of A – Recommended, B – Intermediate, or C – Not Recommended. The *Consumer Bulletin Annual*, published in September, provides a summary of previous product ratings, together with information and advice on current consumer topics. (See Figures 3 and 4.)

BLENDERS

Electric blenders of the same general design as those now being sold have been on the market for over three decades. Most of the changes that have been made over the years have involved only styling and convenience features.

For the present report CR tested 13 blenders, with prices ranging from under $15 to nearly $40. We found that little correlation existed between price and performance. The more expensive models do, generally, have more motor speeds, have fancier styling, and are equipped with timers.

The blenders tested all had multi-speed motors; the number of speeds ranged from three on the *Braun* to 20 on the *Sunbeam*. Apparently the manufacturers feel that a large number of closely spaced speeds is good for sales appeal. However, a moderate number of fairly widely spaced speeds may be equally as useful to the homemaker.

Most of the blenders in this report claimed to have "solid state" speed controls. This term, undoubtedly intended to give the impression that the blenders employ the very latest in electronic technology, was found usually to mean only that a single tiny (and inexpensive) diode is used in the motor control circuit. Use of the diode can double the number of speeds available from a motor. Other than being cheaper than other methods of varying the motor speed, use of the diode seems to have no special advantage. The *Sanyo* blender had another form of solid-state speed control, which provided an infinite number of speeds.

Many blending operations are accomplished in a few seconds, and it is often necessary to stop the blender frequently during that time to inspect the results. Therefore, a "momentary" control switch, which turns the blender off when finger pressure is released, is a real convenience. On some of the blenders with this feature, it was usable with only one or two of all the speeds available.

Some models had timers to turn the blender off after a preset period—a feature judged to be of little value in relation to the higher prices of those that have it.

The blade assembly at the bottom of the container was removable on all the blenders except the *Dormeyer*. With a removable blade assembly one can push sticky mixtures out of the container more easily, it is more convenient to clean sticky residue from around the blades, and one can wash the container (if of glass) separately in a dishwasher. Manufacturers generally recommend against putting the blade assembly in a dishwasher, since the blade bearings and parts made of plastic could be damaged.

The removable blade assemblies do have some disadvantages. Blender containers are more difficult to get thoroughly clean by the usual method of turning on the blender with water and detergent in the container, since there is a crevice or recess at the bottom of the container where it is joined to the blade assembly. Leakage is likely if one forgets to tighten the blade assembly securely on the container or if the gasket is not in good condition. (A gasket may deteriorate with time and use.)

The bearing for the spinning blades seems to be a problem area, at least on some blenders. The shaft may rust and bind or freeze in its bearing when a blender is out of use for a few days. With differing degrees of severity, we had this problem with our

CONSUMER BULLETIN   FEBRUARY 1973 / 7

Figure 3. Typical ratings of products, from Consumer Bulletin.

Proctor-Silex, Wards, Sears, and *Hoover* models.

Even with the removable blade assemblies used on most of the blenders tested, it is often difficult or impossible to remove all of the sticky food residue from the bearing area on some blenders without disassembly of the bearing. While repairing a stuck bearing on one apparently clean blender, we found some decomposing food residues beneath the cutter blade assembly.

The *Wards* and *Vornado* blenders came with plastic containers which, the manufacturers say, should not be cleaned in a dishwasher. The plastic containers had the advantage of being much lighter than the glass ones.

The blade assemblies on several of the blenders will fit on standard Mason jar threads. The instruction booklets for some of the blenders to which this applies say that standard-thread jars may be used, but instructions for a few of the others, we find, do not even mention the subject. It would seem that manufacturers should provide a suitable instruction if they feel that the use of ordinary jars is safe. If it is not safe, manufacturers should use a design of the

threads on their blender blade assemblies that will prevent the user from fitting a Mason jar to the threaded ring.

The blenders have caps over a central opening in their lids; the caps can be removed to add more material to the container while the blender is running. We found that one-hand removal of the cap was difficult on some models.

There are various kitchen mixing jobs for which blenders are not at all suited, but there are certain chores nearly any blender will perform acceptably. CR arranged to have the blenders tried out with several recipes, including soup, whipped cream, cake batter, icing, and liver paste. The blenders were also used to grind coffee beans, make peanut butter from whole peanuts, and make coleslaw from cabbage. (See Table I.) The design of the containers and blades of most of the appliances tested seemed to be good for blending some foods, but poor for some other foods.

An annoying problem with most blenders is that the lids often allow some of the contents to escape when "thin" mixtures or thin liquids like orange juice with solids in suspension are used in the blender. We

Table I—Blender performance in various use tests

Brand	Making soup	Peanut butter	Mayonnaise	Cabbage	Whipping cream	Mixing cake batter	Icing	Liver paste	Grinding coffee
Braun MX-32	poor	fair	fair	fair	good	good	fair	fair	poor
Dormeyer DB-7	fair	fair	good	good	good	good	poor	fair	good
Hoover 8975	fair	good	good	good	good	fair	poor	fair	good
Iona B-34, Type 1	good	fair	poor	good	good	good	fair	poor	poor
Panasonic MX-260	good	good	good	good	good	fair	good	fair	good
Penncrest 5677	poor	fair	good	good	good	good	good	poor	good
Sanyo SM-1000P	good	poor	poor	—	good	good	fair	good	poor
SCM Proctor-Silex 81404	good	fair	fair	good	good	good	fair	fair	poor
Sears 400.829500	fair	good	fair	fair	good	good	fair	poor	poor
Sunbeam 777 LW	poor	good	fair	—	good	fair	good	poor	fair
Vornado 140	poor	good	fair	fair	good	good	fair	poor	poor
Wards Signature PR-45808-83A	poor	fair	fair	poor	good	good	poor	poor	poor
Waring 97, 11-183	fair	poor	good	good	good	fair	poor	poor	good

Performance: The container is supposed to hold 6 cups, but the sample tested by CR seemed to have a defect which caused it to have a small leakage around the edge of the lid when the blender was operated with more than about 2 cups of water in the container. With more than about 4½ cups, the leakage was definitely excessive.

The guarantee is for five years, but the terms are similar, in other respects, to those of most of the other guarantees.

PENNCREST, MODEL 5677 (Penneys Cat. No. R 824-1226C) $18.49, plus shipping.

Description: Plastic base. 7 push buttons for speed selection, off button. Container design apparently identical with that of the *Waring.* Weight of container, 3 lb. 2 oz. Cord length, 45 in. Blender UL listed.

on the right side was pushed. Each of the other 3 buttons served for momentary control and also served to turn the blender off. Overall, the controls seemed needlessly confusing. Weight of container, 3 lb. 1 oz. Cord length, 42 in. Blender UL listed.

Performance: In the test for usable capacity, no significant leakage occurred when the container was filled to the claimed capacity of 5 cups. Sometimes a few drops would escape around the center cap, but the base remained dry. Sometimes the separate blade assembly would stick to the bottom of the container and be hard to remove. When that happened, care had to be taken to avoid stabbing one's thumb with the end of a blade when the assembly did suddenly come off the container. No test for electrical safety with the container overfilled was carried out on this blender.

trol switch, which could be used with only 2 speeds. Booklet does not tell whether container is of heat-resistant glass. Widemouth jars, carefully inspected for defects, may be used on the blender. (Proctor-Silex recommends that only "tempered" jars be used.) Weight of container, 3 lb. 12 oz. Cord length, 39 in. Blender UL listed.

Performance: The graduations on the container go up to 6 cups, but in the test for useful capacity the container was found to hold only 5 cups without excessive spillage. Stability of container on base, only fair. Unusual two-gasket seal between container and blade assembly made removal of the blades comparatively difficult. When the blender was left unattended for a few days, it was found that the blade shaft had rusted and could hardly be turned. Attempting to start the blender then had the effect of unscrewing the bear-

Figure 3. Cont'd

ELECTRIC TYPEWRITERS

Before you purchase any typewriter, type with it at the store, if possible. Type a half page or more, not just one sentence, to see how comfortable the machine is to use. You should be able to determine quickly if the keyboard is satisfactory for *your* touch.

If the typewriter has a power carriage return, note its operation. Is it smooth, fast, and quiet? If not, don't buy it.

Also check the electric backspace, if the typewriter is equipped with one. Does it operate smoothly and quietly? If not, don't buy.

Does the typewriter have a touch control? All electric typewriters should have touch controls to provide a range of key pressures to meet the needs of different individuals. Make sure that the control actually produces a useful effect. Then check and adjust it until the machine seems best suited to your personal touch. If you cannot adjust the machine to suit your touch, don't buy it.

Check to see if the platen is removable. A removable platen allows the user to clean quickly the rollers, paper meter, and platen of ink, correction liquids, erasure grit, and dust. Is the paper meter movable or stationary? A movable paper meter makes cleaning easier. All machines were designed for operation on line voltage of 120 volts a.c., 60 Hz (cycles) and are all listed by the Underwriters' Laboratories. Prices given are "list prices" and in most cases include a carrying case.

Portables with manual carriage return

A. RECOMMENDED

Penncrest, Concord 10 (J. C. Penney Co., Inc., Subdivision 641, 1301 Avenue of the Americas, New York, N.Y. 10019) $129. Made in U.S.A.

Weight, with case, 24½ lb. Electrically-operated features: 88-character keyboard, two shift keys, space bar, "automatic" space bar, 3 repeat keys. Manual features: backspace, shift-key lock, margin release, tabulator, set and clear bars. Noise level, moderate. Overall quality of typed pages, very good. Has provision for interchangeable type. 5-yr. guarantee.

Smith-Corona, Corona Seventy (SCM Corp., 299 Park Ave., New York, N.Y. 10017) $144.50 with zippered Naugahyde carrying bag; a vinyl-clad steel carrying case is available at extra cost. Made in U.S.A.

Brand and model	Length, inches	Platen Writing line, inches	Removable for cleaning?	Line spacing*	Backspace key location	Margin release location	Half letter spacing	"Paper meter" movable?
PORTABLES WITH MANUAL CARRIAGE RETURN								
Brother Electric 3000	9³/8	8³/4	no	1 1¹/2 2	right	left	no	no
Penncrest, Concord 10	9¹/8	8³/8	yes	1 2 3	left	right	no	no
Royal Apollo 12	11¹⁵/16	10⁷/8	no	1 1¹/2 2	right	left	no	no
Smith-Corona, Corona Seventy	9¹/8	8³/8	yes	1 2 3	left	right	no	no
Smith-Corona, Coronet Electric 10	9¹/8	8³/8	yes	1 2 3	left	right	no	no
PORTABLES WITH POWER CARRIAGE RETURN								
Adler Satellite 2001	11³/4	11	no	1 1¹/2 2	right	left	yes	yes
Brother Activator 1230	10⁷/8	10⁷/16	no	1 1¹/2 2	left	right	yes	yes
Olivetti Lettera 36	9³/4	8⁷/8	no	1 2 3	right	left	yes	no
Olympia Report Electric	11¹/16	10⁵/16	no	1 1¹/2 2	right	left	yes	no
Penncrest, Concord PCR12	11¹³/16	11	yes	1 2 3	left	right	yes	no
Remington Automatic 612	10¹³/16	10¹/4	no	1 1¹/2 2	left	right	yes	yes
Royal Jupiter 13	13¹/4	11	no	1 1¹/2 2	left	left	no	yes
Smith-Corona, Electra 220	11¹³/16	11¹/16	yes	1 1¹/2 2 2¹/2 3	left	right	yes	no
Wards Signature 812D	10⁷/8	10⁷/16	no	1 1¹/2 2	left	right	yes	yes
OFFICE MACHINES WITH POWER CARRIAGE RETURN								
Hermes 10	13¹/4	12³/4	no	1 1¹/2 2	right	right	no	no
Smith-Corona 500	14³/4	14¹/16	yes	1 2 3	left	right	yes	no
Wards Signature 1013D	12⁷/8	12¹/8	no	1 1¹/2 2 2¹/2 3	left	right	yes	yes

* Half-line spacing is advantageous for those who type a large number of subscripts and exponents.

Figure 4. Typical ratings of products, from Consumer Bulletin Annual.

Weight, with case, 18¼ lb. Electrically-operated features: 84-character keyboard, two shift keys, space bar with repeat function, 3 repeat keys. Manual features: backspace, margin release, tabulator, set and clear bars. Noise level, moderate. Overall quality of typed pages, good. 5-yr. guarantee.

Smith-Corona, Coronet Electric 10 (SCM Corp.) $159.50. Made in U.S.A.

Weight, with case, 24¼ lb. Electrically-operated features: 88-character keyboard, two shift keys, space bar with repeat function, 3 repeat keys. Manual features: backspace, margin release, tabulator with the set and clear bars. Noise level, moderate. Overall quality of typed pages, good. Has provision for interchangeable type. 5-yr. guarantee.

B. INTERMEDIATE

Brother Electric 3000 (Brother International Corporation, 1515 Pitfield Blvd., Montreal 384, Quebec) $129.95. Made in Japan.

Weight, with case, 20¼ lb. Electrically-operated features: 88-character keyboard, 3 repeat keys. Manual features: space bar, auto-space key, margin release, two shift keys, tabulator key, backspace. Tabulator stops are preset for every 10 spaces at the factory, an undesirable feature. Paper release does not lift paper bail off the platen. Noise level, moderate. Overall quality of typed pages, fair. Inserting paper was difficult. The number of features on this typewriter calling for manual operation were found to be a disadvantage. 5-yr. guarantee.

Royal Apollo 12 Electric, Model SP8500 (Royal Typewriter Co., Div. of Litton Business Systems, Inc., 150 New Park Ave., Hartford, Conn. 06106) $119.95. Made in Japan.

Weight, with case, 18¼ lb. Electrically-operated features: 88-character keyboard, two shift keys, 3 repeat keys. Manual features: margin release, backspace, tabulator key, space bar. Tabulator stops are preset for every 10 spaces at the factory, undesirable. Paper release does not lift the paper bail off the platen. Noise level, moderate. Overall quality of typed pages, good. The number of features on this typewriter calling for manual operation were found to be a disadvantage. 5-year guarantee.

Portable electric typewriters with power carriage returns

A. RECOMMENDED

Adler Satellite 2001 (Adler Business Machines, Inc., Div. of Litton Ind., 1600 Route 22, Union, N.Y. 07083) $233.50. Made in Western Germany.

Weight, with case, 31 lb. Electrically-operated features: 88-character keyboard, two shift keys, tabulator space bar with repeat function, 5 repeat keys, backspace. Manual features: margin release, half-space bar, tabulator set-and-clear lever, half-space key. Noise level, moderate. Overall quality of the typed page, good. 1-year guarantee.

Brother Activator 1230 (Brother International Corp., 680 Fifth Ave., New York, N.Y. 10019) $189.95. Made in Japan.

Weight, with case, 26½ lb. Electrically-operated features: 88-character keyboard, backspace, two shift

keys, space bar, repeat spacer, 3 repeat keys. Manual features: half-letter space, tabulator bar with set and clear bars, margin release. Noise level, moderate. Overall quality of the typed page, good. Has provision for interchangeable type. 5-yr. guarantee.

Olympia Report Electric (Olympia USA Inc., Box 22, Somerville, N.J. 08876) $225. Made in Western Germany.

Weight, with case, 30 lb. Electrically-operated features: 88-character keyboard, two shift keys, tabulator key, repeat line-space function, backspace with repeat function, space bar, vertical-space bar with repeat function, 5 repeat keys. Manual features: margin release, half-letter space, set and clear bars, all-clear lever. Noise level, moderate. Overall quality of the typed page, very good. 1-yr. guarantee.

Penncrest Concord PCR12 (J. C. Penney Co., Inc., Subdivision 641, 1301 Avenue of the Americas, New York, N.Y. 10019) $149. Made in U.S.A.

Weight, with case, 26½ lb. Electrically-operated features: 88-character keyboard, two shift keys, space bar, and automatic space bar, 3 repeat keys. Manual features: backspace key, half-space bar, margin release key, tab set and clear, tabulator. Noise level, moderate. Overall quality of the typed page, good. Has provision for interchangeable type. 5-yr. guarantee.

Remington Automatic 612 (Remington Rand, Office Machines Division, 333 Wilson Ave., Norwalk, Conn. 06856) $199.50. Made in U.S.A.

Weight, with case, 26¼ lb. Electrically-operated features: 88-character keyboard, backspace, two shift keys, repeat space bar, space bar, 3 repeat keys. Manual features: half-space key, margin release, tabulator bar, set and clear bars. Noise level, moderate. Overall quality of the typed page, judged fair. Has provision for interchangeable type. 5-yr. guarantee.

Smith-Corona, Electra 220 (SCM Corporation, 299 Park Ave., New York, N.Y. 10017) $238. Made in U.S.A.

Weight, with case, 25½ lb. Electrically-operated features: 88-character keyboard, two shift keys, space bar, power space bar, 3 repeat keys. Manual features: backspace key, margin release, tabulator bar, set and clear bars, half-space bar. Manual ribbon reverse switch on keyboard. Has a pilot light to indicate when the machine is turned on. Noise level, moderate. Overall quality of the typed page, good. Has provision for interchangeable type. 5-yr. guarantee.

Wards Signature 812D (Wards Cat. No. 8157R) $169.99, plus shipping. Made in Japan.

Weight, with case, 25½ lb. Electrically-operated features: 88-character keyboard, backspace, two shift keys, space bar, repeat space bar, 3 repeat keys. Manual features: half-letter spacing, tabulator bar, set and clear bars, margin release. Noise level, moderate. Overall quality of the typed page, good. Power carriage return was judged not to be as smooth as that on other typewriters. Has provision for interchangeable type. 5-yr. guarantee.

B. INTERMEDIATE

Olivetti Lettera 36 (Olivetti Corporation of America, P.O. Box 767, Murray Hill Station, New York, N.Y. 10016) $169.50. Made in Spain.

Weight, with case, 25½ lb. Electrically-operated features: 86-character keyboard, two shift keys, margin

Figure 4. Cont'd

D5   **CONSUMER CREDIT LETTER** National Research Bureau, 221 N. LaSalle St., Chicago, Ill. 60601. Weekly. $36/year.
A weekly news digest of consumer credit facts.

D6   **CONSUMER EDUCATION FORUM** American Council on Consumer Interests, 238 Stanley Hall, University of Missouri, Columbia, Mo. 65201. 3 issues/year. $6/year.
A newsletter-exchange of ideas for consumer educators.

D7   **CONSUMER FINANCE LAW BULLETIN** National Consumer Finance Association, Suite 702, 1000 16th St., N.W., Washington, D.C. 20036. Quarterly. $10/year.
Provides Association members with an authoritative report on current court decisions and rulings, legislative happenings, regulations, and other pertinent matters.

D8   **CONSUMER FINANCE NEWS** National Consumer Finance Association, Suite 601, 1000 16th St., N.W., Washington, D.C. 20036. Monthly. $6/year.
Official magazine of the consumer finance industry sent to members, educators, and libraries. Contents include timely articles on operations, public relations, economics, personnel relations, law, and other related subjects.

D9   **CONSUMER LEGISLATION MONTHLY REPORT** Office for Legislative Affairs, President's Committee on Consumer Interests, Rm. 6026, New Federal Office Bldg. #7, Washington, D.C. 20506. Free.
Provides a comprehensive listing of consumer legislation.

D10 **CONSUMER NEWS** Office of Consumer Affairs, New Executive Office Bldg., Washington, D.C. 20506. Monthly. $1/year.
Began publication in April 1971. Provides reports on what the federal departments and agencies are doing for the consumer. Includes a brief account of the most current government programs to benefit the consumer, as well as up-to-date information on future plans.

D11 **CON$UMER NEW$WEEK** (Formerly *U.S. Consumer*) Consumer News, Inc., 813 National Press Bldg., Washington, D.C. 20004. Weekly. $15/year.

Features news items regarding any matter considered to be of interest to consumers. Also includes tips on shopping and safety.

D12 **CONSUMER REPORTS** Consumers Union, 256 Washington St., Mt. Vernon, N.Y. 10550. Monthly. $8/year.

Presents results of tests on products; ratings are given as acceptable or not acceptable. Reports on consumer matters are also published. The annual *Buying Guide* analyzes and rates products by brand name.

D13 **CONSUMERS DIGEST** 6316 N. Lincoln Ave., Chicago, Ill. 60645. Bimonthly. $7/year.

Compilation of reports on buying, homes, cars, insurance, business, and job opportunities. Includes discount prices on all lines of products as well as shopping tips. There are two *Price Buying Directories* each year that list products at discount prices, with names of dealers honoring the discounts.

D14 **CONSUMER TRENDS** 375 Jackson Ave., St. Louis, Mo. 63130. Semimonthly. $25/year.

Newsletter on consumer credit and financial affairs.

D15 **CO-OP REPORT** Cooperative League of the U.S.A., 59 E. Van Buren St., Chicago, Ill., 60605. Bimonthly. $3/year.

Tells what all types of co-ops, everywhere, are doing.

D16 **EVERYBODY'S MONEY** Credit Union National Association, Inc., Box 431, Madison, Wis. 53701. Quarterly. $1/year.

Presents information on current consumer topics such as health insurance, banking services, mobile homes, and children's clothes.

D17 **FINANCE FACTS** National Consumer Finance Association,

Education Services Division, Suite 601, 1000 16th St., N.W., Washington, D.C. 20036. Monthly. Free.

This publication on consumer financial behavior is provided as a public service by the U.S. finance and loan companies.

D18 **FINANCE FACTS YEARBOOK** National Consumer Finance Association, Educational Services Division, Suite 601, 1000 16th St., N.W., Washington, D.C. 20036. Annual. Free.

Provides facts about consumer financial behavior and the consumer finance business. Includes an interpretive study of statistical facts about the consumer and his job, income, spending habits, money management, credit management, and use of consumer finance company services. The *Yearbook* is prepared as a public service and is a convenient reference source for those who require accurate and current information about the consumer and his finances.

D19 **FOOD AND NUTRITION** Food and Nutrition Service, U.S. Department of Agriculture, Washington, D.C. 20250. Bimonthly. $1/year.

Concerned with all phases of food programs, such as school lunches, food assistance, and food stamps.

D20 **FOOD AND NUTRITION NEWS** National Live Stock and Meat Board, 36 S. Wabash Ave., Chicago, Ill. 60603. 9 issues/ year. Free.

D21 **THE JOURNAL OF CONSUMER AFFAIRS** American Council on Consumer Interests, 238 Stanley Hall, University of Missouri, Columbia, Mo. 65201. Semiannual. $6/year.

Primarily for professionals in consumer affairs and education, the *Journal* disseminates results of consumer-focused research and discusses public issues affecting the consumer.

D22 **JOURNAL OF HOME ECONOMICS** American Home Economics Association, 1600 20th St., N.W., Washington, D.C. 20009. 10 issues/year. $12/year.

Publishes articles on all phases of home economics including consumer education, as well as abstracts and a bibliography of new books.

D23 MONEYSWORTH 110 W. 40th St., New York, N.Y. 10018. Biweekly. $10/year.
Newsletter on consumer products, legislation, finances, books, and general consumer information.

D24 NATIONAL CONSUMERS LEAGUE BULLETIN 1029 Vermont Ave., N.W., Washington, D.C. 20005. Monthly. $10/year.
Discusses current consumer topics.

D25 OF CONSUMING INTEREST Federal-State Reports, Barr Bldg., 910 17th St., N.W., Washington, D.C. 20006. Monthly. $24/year.
This 8-page publication is designed to keep business informed about consumer-related activities in government and industry.

D26 SERVICE: USDA's Report to Consumers U.S. Department of Agriculture, Office of Information, Washington, D.C. 20250. Monthly. Free.
Newsletter of consumer interest. Designed for personnel who work in consumer affairs rather than for mass distribution.

D27 TEACHING TOOLS FOR CONSUMER EDUCATION Educational Services Division, Consumers Union, 256 Washington St., Mt. Vernon, N.Y. 10550. Monthly. $3.50/year.
Newsletter for teachers and other educators that discusses general consumer items, background information on consumer issues, and simple tests or experiments for classroom use.

D28 WHAT'S NEW IN CO-OP INFORMATION Information Department, Cooperative League of the U.S.A., 59 E. Van Buren St., Chicago, Ill. 60605. Bimonthly. Free.
Discusses topics of interest to cooperatives.

TRADE PAPERS AND MAGAZINES

D29 **ADVERTISING AGE** Advertising Publications, Inc., 740 Rush St., Chicago, Ill. 60611. Weekly. $8/year.

D30 **AMERICAN DRUGGIST** 224 W. 57th St., New York, N.Y. 10019. Biweekly. $11/year.

D31 **CLEARINGHOUSE REVIEW** National Clearinghouse for Legal Services, Northwestern University School of Law, 710 N. Lake Shore Dr., Chicago, Ill. 60611. Monthly. Free.
Contains a section on consumer legal actions.

D32 **CONSUMER FINANCE NEWS** National Consumer Finance Association, Suite 601, 1000 16th St., N.W., Washington, D.C. 20036. Monthly. $6/year.

D33 **THE CREDIT WORLD** International Consumer Credit Association, 375 Jackson Ave., St. Louis, Mo. 63130. Monthly. $6/year.

D34 **DRUG & COSMETIC INDUSTRY** 101 W. 31st St., New York, N.Y. 10001. Monthly. $7/year.

D35 **JOURNAL OF MARKETING RESEARCH** American Marketing Association, 230 N. Michigan Ave., Chicago, Ill. 60601. Quarterly. $12/year.

D36 **MERCHANDISING WEEK** 165 W. 46th St., New York, N.Y. 10036. Weekly. $10/year.

D37 **SALES MANAGEMENT** 630 Third Ave., New York, N.Y. 10017. Semimonthly. $15/year.

GENERAL INTEREST AND WOMEN'S MAGAZINES

D38 **AMERICAN HOME** 641 Lexington Ave., New York, N.Y. 10022. Monthly. $4/year.

D39 **BETTER HOMES AND GARDENS** 1716 Locust St., Des Moines, Iowa 50303. Monthly. $4/year.

D40 **BUSINESS WEEK** 330 W. 42nd St., New York, N.Y. 10036. Weekly. $12/year.
The "Personal Business" column contains items of consumer interest.

D41 **CONGRESSIONAL RECORD** United States Congress. Washington, D.C., U.S. Government Printing Office. Daily, when in session. $1.50/month.
Full record of Congressional proceedings. Indexed by names of Congressmen and subjects. Includes a history of bills and resolutions, arranged by number.

D42 **COSMOPOLITAN** 1775 Broadway, New York, N.Y. 10019. Monthly. $7.20/year.

D43 **DUN'S REVIEW** 466 Lexington Ave., New York, N.Y. 10017. Monthly. $7/year.

D44 **FAMILY CIRCLE** 488 Madison Ave., New York, N.Y. 10022. Monthly. $0.25/issue.

D45 **FORBES** 60 Fifth Ave., New York, N.Y. 10011. Semimonthly. $9.50/year.

D46 **FORTUNE** Time and Life Bldg., New York, N.Y. 10020. 14 issues/year. $14/year.
Contains a useful, regular feature on personal finances.

D47 **GOOD HOUSEKEEPING** 959 Eighth Ave., New York, N.Y. 10019. Monthly. $5/year.
The "Speaker for the House" column gives news and opinions on products, advertisements, and services.

D48 **HOUSE AND GARDEN** 420 Lexington Ave., New York, N.Y. 10017. Monthly. $6/year.

D49 **HOUSE AND HOME** 300 W. 42nd St., New York, N.Y. 10036. Monthly. $6/year.

D50 **HOUSE BEAUTIFUL** 250 W. 55th St., New York, N.Y. 10019. Monthly. $7/year.

D51 **THE KIPLINGER WASHINGTON LETTER** 1729 H St., N.W., Washington, D.C. 20006. Weekly. $24/year.

D52 **LADIES HOME JOURNAL** 641 Lexington Ave., New York, N.Y. 10022. Monthly. $4/year.

D53 **McCALL'S** 230 Park Ave., New York, N.Y. 10017. Monthly. $3.95/year.
The "Right Now" column is a newsletter for women.

D54 **THE NATION** 333 Sixth Ave., New York, N.Y. 10014. Weekly. $12.50/year.

D55 **NATIONAL OBSERVER** 200 Burnett Rd., Chicopee, Mass. 01021. Weekly. $7/year.

D56 **NATION'S BUSINESS** 1615 H St., N.W., Washington, D.C. 20006. Monthly. $26.75/3 years.

D57 **NEW REPUBLIC** 1244 19th St., N.W., Washington, D.C. 20006. Weekly. $12/year.

D58 **NEWSWEEK** 444 Madison Ave., New York, N.Y. 10022. Weekly. $14/year.

D59 **NEW YORK TIMES MAGAZINE** 229 W. 43rd St., New York, N.Y. 10036. Weekly; in Sunday *Times*.

D60 **READER'S DIGEST** Pleasantville, N.Y. 10570. Monthly. $3.97/year.

D61 **REDBOOK** 230 Park Ave., New York, N.Y. 10017. Monthly. $3.95/year.

D62   **TIME**   Rockefeller Center, New York, N.Y. 10020. Weekly. $10/year.

D63   **U.S. NEWS AND WORLD REPORT**   2300 N St., N.W., Washington, D.C. 20037. Weekly. $12/year.
"News You Can Use in Your Personal Planning" column is of consumer interest.

D64   **THE WASHINGTON MONTHLY**   1150 Connecticut Ave., N.W., Washington, D.C. 20036. Monthly. $10/year.
Purpose is to illuminate the American political system with disciplined fact-finding and analysis.

D65   **WOMAN'S DAY**   One Astor Pl., New York, N.Y. 10036. Monthly. $0.25/issue.

Organizations

Federal Government

"All levels of government have important and unique roles in consumer protection. The Federal Government must set national product standards, provide testing and enforcement, and maintain clearinghouses of information."[1]

This Directory attempts to list alphabetically the federal agencies that are primarily concerned with these roles as they pertain to consumer affairs. The descriptions of consumer activities were taken directly from information provided by the agencies and include addresses, telephone numbers, and selected publications.

Many government agencies have regional representation, and some of these are included in Directory F under the appropriate states. Local telephone directories may list additional offices under the heading "U.S. Government."

Additional sources of information may be found in the *Guide to Federal Consumer Services* (see A42) issued by the Office of Consumer Affairs, Executive Office of the President. The *United States Government Organization Manual* (see A69) provides information about all government agencies, including those with consumer interests.

E1   CIVIL AERONAUTICS BOARD (CAB) 1825 Connecticut Ave., N.W., Washington, D.C. 20428.

CAB's Office of Consumer Affairs examines airline customers' complaints to determine and report on the major causes of

---

[1] Council of State Governments. *Consumer Protection in the States.* Lexington, Ky., the Council, December 1970, p. 1.

dissatisfaction. Monthly tabulations of these complaints are available from the Publications Section, CAB. Complaints should be addressed to the Office of Consumer Affairs, Room 1018, CAB. Round-the-clock telephone service has been instituted by CAB's Office of Consumer Affairs. The number is 202-382-7735.

E2 **THE CONGRESS OF THE UNITED STATES** The Capitol, Washington, D.C. 20510.

Numerous Senate and House committees are or have been involved with hearings on legislation concerning consumers. Some of the major committees and subcommittees are listed below:

HOUSE

Commerce Committee, Public Health and Environment Subcommittee.

Committee on Banking and Currency and the Subcommittee on Consumer Affairs.

Committee on District of Columbia and the Subcommittee on Business and Commerce.

Committee on Government Operations.

Committee on Interstate and Foreign Commerce and the Subcommittee on Commerce and Finance.

SENATE

Committee on Banking and Currency, Subcommittee on Financial Institutions.

Committee on Government Operations, Subcommittee on Executive Reorganization and Government Research.

Committee on the Judiciary, Small Business Subcommittee; Subcommittee on Antitrust and Monopoly; Subcommittee on Financial Institutions.

Select Committee on Commerce, Consumer Subcommittee.

Special Committee on the Aging, Subcommittee on Frauds and Misrepresentations Affecting the Elderly.

The following are examples of publications issued by the committees:

U.S. Congress, House, Committee on Government Operations. *Consumer Information Responsibilities of the Federal Government.* Hearings Before Special Studies Subcommittee. 90th Cong., 2nd sess., June 27–29, 1967.

U.S. Congress, House, Committee on Government Operations. *Government Rejected Consumer Items.* Hearings Before Special Studies Subcommittee. 90th Cong., 2nd sess., April 2–3, 1968.

U.S. Congress, House, Committee on Government Operations. *Organizing Federal Consumer Activities. Part I.* Hearings Before the Subcommittee on Executive Reorganization. 91st Cong., 1st sess., September 16–18, 1969; November 13–14, 1969. *Part II.* 91st Cong., 2nd sess., April 13 and 17, 1970.

U.S. Congress, Senate, Committee on Government Operations. *Federal Role in Consumer Affairs.* Hearings Before the Subcommittee on Executive Reorganization and Government Research. 91st Cong., 2nd sess., January 21–22 and February 6, 1970.

Copies of bills and reports are available from the House and Senate Document Rooms; hearings, from the appropriate House or Senate Committee or Subcommittee. The "Calendar" of House and Senate activities is a schedule of upcoming hearings and can be used as a checklist. The *Congressional Record* publishes the official proceedings of the Congress and is issued daily when Congress is in session. The "Daily Digest" at the back summarizes the proceedings of that day. The *Congressional Directory* provides information about the members of Congress and lists all committees, with membership of each. See E17 for a discussion of the *Consumer Legislative Monthly Report*, issued by the Office of Consumer Affairs, Executive Office of the President, and Figure 5 for a sample of a typical comparative analysis of proposed legislation as prepared by the Chamber of Commerce of the United States.

CONSUMER PROTECTION AGENCY

COMPARATIVE ANALYSIS OF S. 707 (93rd CONGRESS) AND S. 3970 (92nd CONGRESS)

	S. 707	S. 3970
Section 201 - Structure	Establishes independent non-regulatory Consumer Protection Agency (CPA) headed by an Administrator appointed by the President and confirmed by Senate for a four-year term coterminous with that of the President.	Same except that Agency would be headed by three-member commission in the Executive Branch.
Section 203 - Intervention	CPA may intervene in all formal agency proceedings affecting "important" consumer interest. Bill expresses preference for less than full party status whenever possible. CPA may also participate in informal agency actions by presenting "relevant informa- tion, briefs and arguments" orally or in writing to agency officials. Participa- tion may not be simultaneous with that of other persons. When participating in informal activities CPA must have "full opportunity" to present its views.	Same CPA intervention in formal agency proceedings except proceeding must only affect consumer interest, not "important" consumer interest. CPA participation in informal activities must be equal to that of any person outside of the agency which is apparently more extensive than the "full opportunity" to present views in S. 707.
Section 204 - Judicial Review	Grants CPA standing to seek or intervene in review of agency actions if CPA deter- mines that a substantial consumer interest is involved. Where CPA did not partici- pate in the proceeding below, it must petition for rehearing before instituting court review if such a petition is "required by law of any person".	Same except that bill does not give CPA sole discretion to determine if a review proceeding affects the consumer interest. Instead, this is a question subject to normal court review. Also, CPA must petition for rehearing before seeking court review if such a petition is "authorized" by law, whether or not it is required or optional.

Figure 5. Comparative Analysis of Consumer Protection Agency legislation pending before the 92nd Congress and the 93rd Congress.

E3 **DEPARTMENT OF AGRICULTURE (USDA)** 4th St. and Independence Ave., S.W., Washington, D.C. 20250 (Telephone: 202-737-4142).

USDA acquires and disseminates information on agricultural subjects and performs research, education, conservation, marketing, regulatory work, agricultural adjustment, surplus disposal, and rural development. Due to the volume of consumer information published and distributed by the Department, several of its Divisions and Services are discussed separately below.

Consumer and Marketing Service. Its mission is to service, regulate, improve, and protect the nation's food marketing system—to help give force to the principle that our supply of food and other farm products shall move from producer to consumer quickly, efficiently, safely, and with fairness to all. It administers broad inspection, marketing, regulatory, and related programs. Information concerning supply and demand, prices, movements, quality, conditions, and other data in specific markets and marketing areas is collected and disseminated. The Service publishes *Federal-State Market News Report—A Directory of Services Available* (C&M-21), which lists market news reports of the Service. *Available Publications of USDA's Consumer and Marketing Service* (C&MS-53) lists all other Service publications. Many of the publications are in Spanish.

Food and Nutrition Service. This Service provides to the citizenry information on nutrition and food programs provided by USDA including the National School Lunch Program, School Breakfast Program, Food Stamp Program, Commodity Distribution Program, Equipment Program (to expand or initiate school food service), and Special Milk Program. For information concerning any of these programs, contact the appropriate state agency or the responsible USDA Division or Service.

Division of Home Economics—Federal Extension Service. The Division provides a "Low Income Teaching Kit on Credit," which contains useful leaflets on determining the actual dollar cost of credit and where to obtain and how to use credit.

Examples of some of the many publications of the Department are:

Color Filmstrips and Slide Sets of the USDA. Washington, D.C., USDA, Office of Information, Photography Division. AF 1107. Free.

Consumers All: the Yearbook of Agriculture. Washington, D.C., U.S. Government Printing Office, 1965. $2.75. Provides information about buying, using, or making food, clothing, household furnishings, and equipment; managing money; caring for yards, gardens, and houses; bettering communities; using leisure time; and staying healthy. This popular book has been published under other titles, including *The Consumer's Handbook* by Paul McKenna Fargis, New York, Hawthorne Books, 1967, $6.95.

A *Consumer's Guide to USDA Services.* Washington, D.C., U.S. Government Printing Office, June 1966. Miscellaneous Publication No. 959. $0.20.

Consumer's Quick Credit Guide. Washington, D.C., U.S. Government Printing Office, 1964. $0.05.

A *Guide to Budgeting for the Young Couple.* Agricultural Research Service. Washington, D.C., U.S. Government Printing Office, 1964. Home and Garden Bulletin No. 98. $0.10.

E4 **DEPARTMENT OF HOUSING AND URBAN DEVELOPMENT (HUD)** 451 7th St., S.W., Washington, D.C. 20410 (Telephone: 202-655-4000).

HUD assists in providing for sound development of the nation's communities and metropolitan areas. It issues pamphlets such as *Consumer Protection, Interstate Land Sales; Home Mortgage Insurance; Home Counseling Service; Fixing Up Your Home;* and a catalog of films entitled *Urban Outlook.*

E5 **DEPARTMENT OF JUSTICE** Consumer Affairs Section Washington, D.C. 20530 (Telephone: 202-737-8200).

This Section is responsible for processing cases referred to the Department by three agencies—Federal Trade Commission, Food and Drug Administration, and Department of Agriculture —that have primary consumer protection responsibilities. The Department of Justice has cooperated in the sponsorship of conferences on consumer protection. An example is the National Conference on Antitrust Problems and Consumer and Investor Protection, cosponsored by the Council of State Governments in 1961.

E6 **DEPARTMENT OF LABOR** 14th St. and Constitution Ave., N.W., Washington, D.C. 20210 (Telephone: 202-393-2420).

The Department of Labor administers and enforces statutes designed to advance the public interest by promoting the welfare of wage earners, improving their working conditions, and advancing their opportunities for profitable employment. The Bureau of Labor Statistics issues the *Consumer Price Index* monthly and the *Wholesale Price Index* quarterly.

E7 **DEPARTMENT OF TRANSPORTATION (DOT)** 400 7th St., S.W., Washington, D.C. 20590 (Telephone: 202-426-4000).

DOT is responsible for "developing national transportation policies and programs conducive to the provision of fast, safe, efficient, and convenient transportation." The mission of its Office of Consumer Affairs is to formulate and recommend departmental policies and courses of action in the field of consumer interests and to advise the Assistant Secretary for Safety and Consumer Affairs on departmental relationships with consumer groups and organizations. The Office of Standards Enforcement, Motor Vehicle Programs, National Highway Traffic Safety Administration is responsible for performing activities relating to compliance with the requirements of the National Traffic and Motor Vehicle Safety Act and the prescribed motor vehicle safety standards. To aid in the enforcement of all safety standards, the Office examines records, reports, and other information from manufacturers; conducts the required tests, inspections, and investigations as necessary; and develops information with respect to noncompliance. DOT issues monthly reports on the status of the Standards Enforcement Test Program.

E8 **FEDERAL DEPOSIT INSURANCE CORPORATION (FDIC)** 550 17th St., N.W., Washington, D.C. 20429 (Telephone: 202-393-8400).

FDIC provides deposit insurance coverage to banks and administers, in part, truth-in-lending legislation. It publishes such items as *Offices of Operating Banks Not Insured by the Federal Deposit Insurance Corporation.*

E9 **FEDERAL RESERVE SYSTEM, Board of Governors** 20th St. and Constitution Ave., N.W., Washington, D.C. 20551 (Telephone: 202-737-1100).

The Board of Governors determines general monetary, credit, and operating policies for the Federal Reserve System and formulates rules and regulations necessary to carry out the purposes of the Federal Reserve Act. The Board distributes a pamphlet, *What You Ought to Know About Truth-in-Lending.* A filmstrip on the Truth-in-Lending Act is available from System headquarters and Federal Reserve Banks and their branches.

E10 **FEDERAL TRADE COMMISSION (FTC)** Washington, D.C. 20580.

The Federal Trade Commission is a regulatory agency that protects the public interest from unfair methods of competition in business and proscribes unfair acts or deceptive practices in commerce. Its fundamental purpose is to guide business, rather than to prosecute violators. The Bureau of Consumer Protection receives complaints from individuals and groups. Numerous publications and a series of consumer bulletins and buyer's guides are available from FTC's Division of Legal and Public Records and the U.S. Government Printing Office (GPO). Several of these are *List of Common Deceptions, Look for That Label, Mail Order Insurance, Don't Be Gypped,* and *Unordered Merchandise.* FTC publications may also be seen in GPO depository libraries.

E11 FOOD AND DRUG ADMINISTRATION (FDA) 5600 Fishers Lane, Rockville, Md. 20852.

FDA protects the health of American consumers by ensuring that foods are safe, pure, and wholesome; drugs and therapeutic devices are safe and effective; cosmetics are harmless; and that all of these products are honestly and informatively labeled and packaged. FDA is also empowered to see that dangerous household products carry adequate warnings for safe use and are properly labeled; counterfeiting of drugs is stopped; unsafe toys are banned; and that hazards incident to the use of other types of consumer products are reduced. Its Bureau of Product Safety develops and conducts programs to reduce injuries and eliminate hazards associated with consumer products, toys, flammable fabrics, and hazardous substances and to inform consumers of such hazards. A *Directory of State Officials Charged with the Enforcement of Food, Drug, Cosmetic, and Food Laws* is available free from FDA. Free publications and posters also are available from the FDA Distribution and Mailing Unit, 200 C St., S.W., Washington, D.C. 20204. For educational audiovisual films, filmstrips, and other materials, write to DCA Educational Products, Inc., 4865 Stenton Ave., Philadelphia, Pa. 19144. A 28-minute color film, "The Health Fraud Racket," is available on free, short-term loan from the National Medical Audiovisual Center (Annex), Attn: Distribution, Station K, Atlanta, Ga. 30334.

E12 GENERAL SERVICES ADMINISTRATION (GSA), Consumer Product Information Coordinating Center 18th and F Sts., N.W., Washington, D.C. 20405.

GSA's Consumer Product Information Coordinating Center was established in October 1970 to encourage the development and publication of product information resulting from the government's research, development, and procurement activities and to promote public awareness of existing federal publications. The Center publishes and distributes *Consumer Product Information: An Index to Selected Federal Publications of Consumer Interest* quarterly, free of charge. The first issue included published items concerning appliances, automobiles, budget and finance, child care, clothing and fabrics, gardening and land-scaping, health, housing, and food. GSA also operates Federal Information Centers in 26 cities and provides free, long-distance telephone service to consumers in 16 other cities. Centers are located in Albuquerque, Atlanta, Baltimore, Boston, Buffalo, Chicago, Cincinnati, Cleveland, Denver, Detroit, Fort Worth, Honolulu, Kansas City (Missouri), Los Angeles, Miami, Minne-apolis, New Orleans, New York, Newark (New Jersey), Phila-delphia, Pittsburgh, Portland (Oregon), St. Louis, San Diego, San Francisco, and Seattle.

E13 HEALTH SERVICES AND MENTAL HEALTH AD-MINISTRATION (HSMHA), Department of Health, Edu-cation, and Welfare   330 Independence Ave., S.W., Washing-ton, D.C. 20201 (Telephone: 202-962-2246).

This agency provides leadership and direction for general and mental health programs and services. It is concerned with the development of comprehensive health care and maintenance systems which are adequately financed and responsive to the needs of all citizens. Among its publications are *Services for Health—HSMHA* and *Health Information for International Travel*. Additional titles may be found in the catalog, *Publica-tions of the Health Services and Mental Health Administration*. Films on mental health problems, drug abuse, and alcoholism are available from the National Institute of Mental Health Film Collection, National Audiovisual Center, National Archives and Records Service (GSA), Washington, D.C. 20409.

E14 NATIONAL AUDIOVISUAL CENTER, National Archives and Records Services   Washington, D.C. 20409.

The Center provides information about, and sells copies of, audiovisual materials published by agencies and other units of the Federal Government. A catalog of films, slides, and other materials is available free.

E15 NATIONAL BUREAU OF STANDARDS (NBS), Depart-ment of Commerce   Washington, D.C. 20234 (Telephone: 301-921-1000).

As the nation's central measurement laboratory, NBS assures maximum application of physical and engineering sciences for the advancement of technology in industry and commerce. It serves the interests of the consumer in three basic areas; measurement, product and safety standards, and information. The *Consumer Information Series* pamphlets are based on material developed in the technical programs carried out by NBS. These booklets are available from the Superintendent of Documents, U.S. Government Printing Office, Washington, D.C. 20402. A list of technical publications and a film catalog also are available from NBS.

E16   **NATIONAL BUSINESS COUNCIL FOR CONSUMER AFFAIRS, Department of Commerce**   14th St., N.W., Washington, D.C. 20230 (Telephone: 202-783-9200).

The Council was established August 5, 1971 to emphasize and encourage voluntary activity by business firms in meeting their responsibilities to the consumer. Thus, the Council serves as a catalyst for the development of constructive industry actions in the field of consumer affairs. There are seven subcouncils: Advertising and Promotion, Packaging and Labeling, Warranties and Guarantees, Credit and Other Terms of Sale, Performance and Services, Product Safety, and Complaints and Remedies.

E17   **OFFICE OF CONSUMER AFFAIRS**   Executive Office of the President, New Executive Office Bldg., Washington, D.C. 20506 (Telephone: 202-395-3682).

The Office of Consumer Affairs was established February 24, 1971 and replaced the President's Committee on Consumer Interests. It is responsible for planning and policy making in consumer affairs and is a focal point for government efforts to aid people who buy. There is a 12-member Consumer Advisory Council to provide guidance with respect to policy matters, effectiveness of federal programs and operations, and problems of consumers. The Office issues a cumulative *Consumer Legislative Monthly Report, 92nd Congress* that lists, by subject area, all bills introduced in the Senate or House, including proposed legislation submitted to Congress by the President. The *Report* is indexed by bill number. Included is a listing of "Scheduled Federal Departmental, Agency, or Commission Notices and Hearings of Consumer Interest." The Office has compiled and distributed *Major Consumer Laws Enacted by the 89th, 90th, and 91st Congresses*, as well as lists of private consumer groups and consumer offices in state, county, and city governments. It also publishes *Consumer News*, a monthly newsletter; *Consumer Education Bibliography*; *Suggested Guidelines for Consumer Education—Grades K-12*; *Forming Consumer Organizations*; *Guide to Federal Consumer Services*; and numerous brochures directed at specific consumer problems, often based on inquiries and complaints received. A number of these brochures are printed in Spanish.

E18 **OFFICE OF ECONOMIC OPPORTUNITY (OEO)** 1200 19th St., N.W., Washington, D.C. 20506 (Telephone: 202-254-5000).

OEO was established to strengthen, supplement, and coordinate efforts to eliminate poverty through opportunities for education and employment. It provides grants for numerous projects, including aid to consumers. Its Community Action Program provides assistance to public and private institutions in dealing with poverty, holds conferences on consumer affairs and poverty, and sponsors studies of buying clubs and cooperatives and problems of the poor. An effort has been made to provide co-op manager's manuals and organizational and operational handbooks. Speakers and films are available from the Plans Branch, IP&M Division, Office of Public Affairs, Room 207. The *Operations Manual—Co-op Stores and Buying Clubs*, prepared by the Inner City Project (Checchi and Company), is a training guide for the Mid-Atlantic Region of OEO and is available from OEO free of charge. The *Catalog of Federal Domestic Assistance* gives a description of the Federal Government's domestic programs to assist the American people in furthering their social and economic progress. It explains the nature and purpose of programs, specifies major eligibility requirements and tells where to apply, and lists printed materials available. There are 10 OEO regional offices from which information may be obtained: JFK Federal Building, Boston, Mass. 02203; 26 Federal Plaza, New York, N.Y. 10007; U.S. Customs House, Philadelphia, Pa. 19106; 730 Peachtree St., N.E., Atlanta, Ga. 30308; 623 Wabash Avenue, Chicago, Ill. 60605; 1100 Commerce St., Dallas, Tex. 75202; 911 Walnut St., Kansas City, Mo. 64106; Federal Office Building, Denver, Colo. 80202; 100 McAllister St., San Francisco, Calif. 94102; and 1321 Second Ave., Seattle, Wash. 98101.

E19 **OFFICE OF EDUCATION (OE), Department of Health, Education, and Welfare** 400 Maryland Ave., S.W., Washington, D.C. 20202 (Telephone: 202-963-1110).

OE collects statistics and facts that show the condition and progress of education, distributes information to aid in the establishment and maintenance of efficient school systems, and promotes the cause of education. It publishes the *Education Directory, American Education,* and *Research in Education.*

E20 **SOCIAL SECURITY ADMINISTRATION** 6401 Security Blvd., Baltimore, Md. 21235 (Telephone: 301-944-5000).

This agency administers the federal retirement, survivors, disability, and health insurance programs. The booklet, *Your Social Security,* explains eligibility and benefits. Films are available, on loan, to public or private groups and organizations through local Social Security Offices or from the Office of Public Affairs at the above address.

E21 **U.S. GOVERNMENT PRINTING OFFICE (GPO)** Superintendent of Documents, Washington, D.C. 20402.

The Government Printing Office—upon orders of Congress, the Departments, and Offices of the Federal Government—prints, binds, distributes, and sells government publications. A list of depository libraries maintaining copies of all government publications is available from GPO. Bookstores are located in Washington, D.C.; Atlanta, Georgia; Boston, Massachusetts; Chicago, Illinois; Dallas, Texas; Kansas City, Missouri; and Los Angeles and San Francisco, California. Information currently available to the consumer is listed in the following three GPO publications:

Consumer Information Price List 86. Includes items available from the various Federal Government offices and sold by GPO. Contains sections on appliances, clothing, fabrics, family finances, credit, food, health, safety, house, and home. Appendix A lists consumer information publications available in Spanish. Appendix B lists information specifically designed for senior citizens.

Monthly Catalog, United States Government Publications. A listing of all documents printed during the previous month, where they are available, and prices. Arranged in alphabetical order by issuing body—whether Congressional or Departmental —with subject index.

Selected Publications of the United States Government. A semimonthly listing of new publications for sale by the Superintendent of Documents. Includes annotations and prices. Free.

State: Government and Private

Each state has agencies—both public and private—geared to assist consumers. The listings in this Directory include the following:

State Government Agencies. Consumer protection in most states is usually the responsibility of the State Attorney General, and consumer protection offices have been established in that department. Other states maintain offices directly under the Governor. In addition, the Departments of Agriculture (and its Extension Service), Commerce, and Education are active in the consumer area and publish numerous items of direct interest to the consumer. Publications issued by the State Government agencies are listed and indexed in the *Monthly Checklist of State Publications* (see A48).

County and City Government Agencies. There are many consumer offices at these levels of government, some of which have enacted their own laws to protect the consumer.

Federal Government Agencies. Many of the federal departments listed in Directory E have regional or area offices. These are listed under the individual states.

Private or Independent Organizations. In many areas, citizens have formed groups to help themselves. These groups are usually voluntary community efforts. Many businesses, trade associations, and manufacturers have also established consumer affairs committees to assist and advise their customers. Universities are excellent sources of consumer information, both through their various departments—such as home economics—and through university extension services. Some universities offer consumer education programs and publish consumer guides for their students.

This Directory is arranged alphabetically by state. The listings for each state are arranged alphabetically by the city in which an agency is located.

Agency entries are based entirely on information received in response to the authors' requests. Therefore, the same types of offices may not be listed in every state. This does not mean, however, that similar offices do not exist.

Many states have research units, legislative councils, etc., that have published reports on consumer matters in that state. These documents and books are mentioned at the end of the respective state listings.

One source of general information applicable to all states is The Council of State Governments. The Council is a joint agency of the 50 state governments—created, supported, and directed by them. It conducts research on state programs and problems; maintains an information service available to state agencies, officials, and legislators; issues a variety of publications (including *Consumer Protection in the States*); assists in federal-state liaison; promotes regional and state-local cooperation; and provides staff for affiliated organizations. Its headquarters office is located at Iron Works Pike, Lexington, Ky. 40505. Other offices are located at 36 W. 44th St., New York, N.Y. 10036; 1313 E. 60th St., Chicago, Ill. 60637; 830 W. Peachtree St., N.W., Atlanta, Ga. 30308; 211 Sutter St., San Francisco, Calif. 94108; and 1735 DeSales St., N.W., Washington, D.C. 20036.

ALABAMA

F1   ALABAMA CONSUMER ASSOCIATION   P.O. Box 1372, Birmingham 35201.

F2   ATTORNEY GENERAL   State Administration Bldg., Montgomery 36104.

ALASKA

F3   **ALASKA CONSUMER COUNCIL**   833 18th St., W., Anchorage 99501.

F4   **ATTORNEY GENERAL OF ALASKA**   Pouch K, State Capitol, Juneau 99801 (Telephone: 907-586-5391).

F5   **KENAI PENINSULA CONSUMER COUNCIL**   Box 2940, Kenai 99611.

ARIZONA

F6   **CONSUMER FRAUD DIVISION, State of Arizona**   159 State Capitol Bldg., Phoenix 85007 (Telephone: 602-271-4266).
     The Consumer Fraud Division was created as a unit of the State Attorney General's office in March 1967. A complaint to this Division will give an Assistant Attorney General or an investigator the opportunity to process the matter through its files and investigation procedures. It issues a *Guide to Consumer Protection* aimed at alerting the consumer to fraud and deception.

F7   **ARIZONA CONSUMERS COUNCIL**   6840 Camino de Michael St., Tucson 85718 (Telephone: 602-884-1495).

ARKANSAS

F8   **ASSISTANT ATTORNEY GENERAL, Consumer Protection** Justice Bldg., Little Rock 72201 (Telephone: 501-376-3871).

CALIFORNIA

F9   **AGRICULTURAL EXTENSION SERVICE**   University of California, Public Service, 90 University Hall, Berkeley 94720.
     A catalog listing many free publications on family and con-

sumer topics is available. Some of these publications are: *Maximum Credit Charges Allowed in California*; *Before You Sign a Contract*; *Buying on Time*; *Credit*; *Shop for Your Loan*; and *Use Credit Wisely*.

F10   ASSOCIATION OF CALIFORNIA CONSUMERS University of California, Institute of Industrial Relations, 2521 Channing Way, Berkeley 94704 (Telephone: 415-642-0323).

F11   AMERICAN CONSUMERS COUNCIL 9720 Wilshire Blvd., Beverly Hills 90212 (Telephone: 213-271-8141).

F12   DOWNTOWN BUSINESS ASSOCIATION CONSUMERS BUREAU 304 Broadway, Chico 95926 (Telephone: 916-343-3754).

F13   ASSOCIATION OF CALIFORNIA CONSUMERS Los Angeles and Orange County Chapters, 644 Tiger Tail Rd., Los Angeles 90049 (Telephone: 213-879-0154).

F14   CONSUMER PROTECTION COMMITTEE OF THE CITY OF LOS ANGELES Rm. 303, City Hall, Los Angeles 90013 (Telephone: 213-485-3304).

F15   DEPARTMENT OF JUSTICE, Consumer Protection Unit 600 State Bldg., Los Angeles 90012 (Telephone: 213-620-2494).
      "The Big Con," a 27-minute color film on frauds, is available on a free, loan basis.

F16   FDA DISTRICT OFFICE 1521 W. Pico Blvd., Los Angeles 90015.

F17   FTC FIELD OFFICE Rm. 13209, 11000 Wilshire Blvd., Los Angeles 90024 (Telephone: 213-824-7575).
      Citizens may receive information pertaining to advertising or labeling of merchandise and products and on truth-in-lending. Many pamphlets are available, including *Advice for Persons Who Are Considering an Investment in a Franchise Business*.

F18 **INDEPENDENT GARAGE OWNERS OF CALIFORNIA (IGO)** Suite 33, 672 S. Lafayette Park Pl., Los Angeles 90057 (Telephone: 213-387-2133).

IGO sponsors the Committees on Auto Repairs and Service in an attempt to establish, in California, a self-policing system whereby the entire industry can protect itself from restrictive legislation and from fraudulent operators within its own ranks. The Committees furnish expert evaluations of complaints from consumers about auto repairs. Where complaints are valid, they discuss the problem with the shop involved and urge the owner to make the job good. The Committees also are prepared to offer expert technical testimony in cases of litigation or prosecution.

F19 **LOS ANGELES CONSUMER PROTECTION COMMITTEE** 107 S. Broadway, Los Angeles 90012 (Telephone: 213-620-2003).

F20 **ASSOCIATION OF POMONA VALLEY CONSUMERS** P.O. Box 2207, Montclair 91763 (Telephone: 714-621-1433).

F21 **ASSOCIATION OF CALIFORNIA CONSUMERS** Rm. 605, 1939 Harrison St., Oakland 94612.

F22 **DIVISION OF CONSUMER AFFAIRS** Department of Weights and Measures, Ventura County, 608 El Rio Dr., Oxnard 93030 (Telephone: 805-487-5511).

F23 **NORTH VALLEY OCCUPATIONAL TRAINING CENTER** Pacoima Skills Center, 13299 Louvre St., Pacoima 91331.

F24 **BAY AREA NEIGHBORHOOD DEVELOPMENT** 4801 Central Ave., Richmond 94804.

This organization offers informational material in its consumer counseling series, advisor leaflets, and cartoon leaflets. The latter also are available in Spanish.

F25 **CONSUMERS COOPERATIVE OF BERKELEY, INC.** 4805 Central Ave., Richmond 94804 (Telephone: 415-526-0440).

F26 ATTORNEY GENERAL OF CALIFORNIA 500 Wells Fargo Bank Bldg., Sacramento 95814 (Telephone: 916-445-4334).

F27 CITIZENS FOR CONSUMER ACTION 4230 DeCosta Ave., Sacramento 95821 (Telephone: 916-483-1403).

F28 CONSUMER AFFAIRS AGENCY The Capitol, Sacramento 95814.

F29 CONSUMER COALITION Suite 212, 1108 O St., Sacramento 95814 (Telephone: 916-447-8926).

F30 DEPARTMENT OF CONSUMER AFFAIRS, State of California 1200 N St., Sacramento 95814 (Telephone: 916-445-4465).

The Department's objectives are to promote and safeguard the interests of the consumer in the marketplace; to protect the public health, general welfare, and safety by licensing only persons and firms of demonstrated knowledge and abilities to perform services for the public; and to discipline those licensees who fail in their public trust. The Department works actively to protect the consumer from unfair or deceptive business practices and from the production, distribution, and sale of any goods or services that may endanger the public health, safety, or welfare. The Division of Consumer Services, located at 1021 O St. (Telephone: 916-445-0660), distributes information concerning the Department, summaries of legislation, items of general interest to the consumer, and listings of consumer education information and consumer associations in California. A brochure on the Department gives names and addresses where complaints can be filed.

F31 DEPARTMENT OF EDUCATION Bureau of Homemaking Education, 721 Capitol Hall, Sacramento 95814.

F32 SACRAMENTO CONSUMER PROTECTION SERVICE 3720 Folsom Blvd., Sacramento 95817 (Telephone: 916-451-2815).

F33 **CONSUMER PANEL OF AMERICA** 1424 Windsor Dr., San Bernardino 92404 (Telephone: 714-885-5393).

F34 **COUNCIL OF STATE GOVERNMENTS,** Western Office 211 Sutter St., San Francisco 94108.

F35 **FDA DISTRICT OFFICE** 518 Federal Office Bldg., 50 Fulton St., San Francisco 94102.

F36 **FTC FIELD OFFICE** 450 Golden Gate Ave., Box 36005, San Francisco 94102 (Telephone: 415-556-1270).
Citizens may receive information pertaining to advertising or labeling of merchandise and products and on truth-in-lending. Many pamphlets are available, including *Advice for Persons Who Are Considering an Investment in a Franchise Business.*

F37 **SAN FRANCISCO CONSUMER PROTECTION COMMITTEE** c/o Department of Justice, 6000 State Bldg., San Francisco 94102 (Telephone: 415-557-2544).

F38 **WESTERN REGION PLENTIFUL FOODS PROGRAM** Consumer and Marketing Service, USDA, Rm. 710, 630 Sansome St., San Francisco 94111 (Telephone: 415-556-4953).

F39 **CALIFORNIA FARMER-CONSUMER INFORMATION COMMITTEE** 740 Hilmar St., Santa Clara 95050 (Telephone: 408-248-7645).

F40 **SANTA CLARA COUNTY DEPARTMENT OF WEIGHTS AND MEASURES AND CONSUMER AFFAIRS** Division of Consumer Affairs, 409 Matthew St., Santa Clara 95050 (Telephone: 408-299-2105).

F41 **REDWOOD ASSOCIATION OF CONSUMERS** 1066 O'Dell La., Santa Rosa 95401 (Telephone: 707-542-7957).

F42 **ASSOCIATION OF CALIFORNIA CONSUMERS** 3030 Bridgeway Bldg., Sausalito 94965 (Telephone: 415-332-3667).

F43   WEST LOS ANGELES COMMUNITY SERVICE OR-
      GANIZATION   11914 Santa Monica Blvd., W. Los Angeles
      90025 (Telephone: 213-820-3002).

PUBLICATIONS:
   *California Laws, Statutes, etc., Agricultural Code, Annotated,
of the State of California.*   Adopted March 15, 1967; effective
November 8, 1967. Annotated and indexed by the publisher's
editorial staff. San Francisco, Bancroft-Whitney Co., 1967.
   *Conference on Consumer Protection in California, Proceed-
ings.*   San Francisco State College, 1962.
   Consumer Food Packaging, a Report.   Sacramento, Assembly
of the State of California, Interim Committee on Agriculture,
1965.

COLORADO

F44   COLORADO CONSUMERS ASSOCIATION, INC.   P.O.
      Box 989, Boulder 80302 (Telephone: 303-444-3776).

F45   ASSISTANT ATTORNEY GENERAL, Office of Consumer
      Affairs   503 Farmers Union Bldg., 1575 Sherman St., Denver
      80203 (Telephone: 303-892-3501).

F46   COLORADO   HOUSEWIVES   ENCOURAGING
      KNOWLEDGE   945 Malley Dr., Denver 80233.

F47   FDA DISTRICT OFFICE   5604 New Customhouse Bldg.,
      20th and California Sts., Denver 80202.

F48   FTC FIELD OFFICE   18013 Federal Office Bldg., 1961
      Stout St., Denver 80202 (Telephone: 303-297-3480).

F49   COOPERATIVE EXTENSION SERVICE   U.S. Depart-
      ment of Agriculture, Colorado State University, Fort Collins
      80521.
         *Popular Publications for the Farmer, Suburbanite, Home-
      maker, Consumer* is offered.

PUBLICATION:

Consumer and Funeral Problems. Legislative Council Report to the Colorado General Assembly. Denver, Committee on Consumer Problems and the Funeral Industry, 1964. Publication 94.

CONNECTICUT

F50 CONNECTICUT CONSUMERS ASSOCIATION, INC. 1016 Broad St., Bridgeport 06611 (Telephone: 203-368-4201).

F51 DEPARTMENT OF CONSUMER PROTECTION, State of Connecticut State Office Bldg., Hartford 06115 (Telephone: 203-566-3388).

The Department, through its separate Divisions, assists the consumer and protects his rights. The Food Division enforces state laws and regulations requiring that foods be safe, wholesome, and honestly and informatively labeled, advertised, and packaged. The Drug, Device, and Cosmetic Division enforces laws that prevent the manufacture or sale of articles that are unsafe, not effective, adulterated, misbranded, or advertised in a false or misleading manner. The Commission of Pharmacy issues licenses to pharmacists, pharmacy interns, retail pharmacies, and retail stores that sell, dispense, and store drugs, medicines, narcotics, poisons, patent medicines, and cosmetics. The Weights and Measures Division ensures the accuracy of all devices used to determine the size, extent, weight, area, or quantity of objects, things, and commodities. The Consumer Frauds Division functions to protect the consuming public from merchandising deceit through enforcement of the statutes provided by the General Assembly.

F52 CONNECTICUT CONSUMER ASSOCIATION P.O. Box 404, Storrs 06268.

The Association provides research information and educational services to consumers and encourages, sponsors, and promotes sound legislation and its enforcement in the interest of the consumer. It operates a speaker's bureau, sponsors workshops and seminars, provides school curriculum materials, assists in organizing area consumer groups, follows up on consumer complaints, and publishes a newsletter, *Consumer's Voice*.

F53 **COOPERATIVE EXTENSION SERVICE** The University of Connecticut, Storrs 06268.

Among the materials offered are: *Consumer Education Bibliography*; *The Food Stamp Program*; *The Door to Door Selling Law*; *The Wage Garnishment Law*; *Licensing and Regulating of Debt Adjustors*; *Credit Cards—Thirty Days to Reality*; *The Sale Price Law*; *Consumer Credit*; and *El Use Del Credito (What Credit Is)*. "Ads Add Up" is a 50-slide and tape presentation pointing out what consumers should know about advertising.

DELAWARE

F54 **DEPARTMENT OF COMMUNITY AFFAIRS AND ECONOMIC DEVELOPMENT** Old State House, Dover 19901 (Telephone: 302-678-4000).

F55 **DEPUTY ATTORNEY GENERAL, Consumer Protection Division** 1206 King St., Wilmington 19801 (Telephone: 302-658-6641).

F56 **DIVISION OF CONSUMER AFFAIRS** 704 Delaware Ave., Wilmington 19801 (Telephone: 302-658-9251, ext. 442).

DISTRICT OF COLUMBIA

F57 **BETTER BUSINESS BUREAU OF METROPOLITAN WASHINGTON** Perpetual Bldg., Washington 20004.

F58 **CONSUMER ASSOCIATION OF THE DISTRICT OF**

COLUMBIA 912 Massachusetts Ave., N.E., Washington 20002.

F59 **CONSUMER PROTECTION CENTER** Urban Law Institute, George Washington University, 714 21st St., N.W., Washington 20006.

This Center was established as part of a clinical experiment for a course on "Problems of the Consumer" and cosponsors a Consumer Help Center with WTTG-TV. The consumer is given appropriate referrals on federal, state, and local levels which will enable him to receive a quick and satisfactory resolution of his problem. Fraudulent and deceptive practices uncovered as a result of complaints are revealed in news broadcasts on WTTG-TV. Complaint referrals are followed up to determine their success, and investigations are under way for sources of new referrals. Law students in the clinical experiment teach consumer awareness classes in the public schools. Four monographs have been written explaining how the course originated, course organization and methodology, and teaching techniques and materials. They are: *Course Organization*, *The Consumer Help Center*, *Consumer Awareness Teaching Materials*, and *Television Programming*.

F60 **COUNCIL OF STATE GOVERNMENTS, Washington Office** 1735 DeSales St., N.W., Washington, 20036.

F61 **D.C. CITYWIDE CONSUMER COUNCIL** 4547 Lee St., N.W., Washington 20019.

F62 **NEIGHBORHOOD CONSUMER INFORMATION CENTER (NCIC)** 3005 Georgia Ave., N.W., Washington 20001.

NCIC investigates and resolves problems of low-income consumers, prepares radio and television consumer-education spots in consultation with the U.S. Office of Consumer Affairs, runs its own complaint department, conducts classes, and operates a speaker's bureau to inform citizens of their consumer rights and to explain unscrupulous business practices. It is supported by private foundations and an Office of Economic Opportunity grant. *Buyers Beware* is a free monthly newsletter reporting on local developments in the areas of consumer education and action.

PUBLICATION:

Report on the City Council Regulations Governing Retail Installment Sales in the District of Columbia. District of Columbia Ad Hoc Committee on Consumer Affairs. Washington, D.C., Government of the District of Columbia City Council, 1969.

FLORIDA

F63 **AMERICAN CONSUMERS ASSOCIATION, INC.** P.O. Box 24141, Fort Lauderdale 33307 (Telephone: 305-933-3882).

F64 **DADE COUNTY CONSUMERS COUNCIL** 1741 S.W. 4th St., Fort Lauderdale 33312.

F65 **DIVISION OF CONSUMER AFFAIRS, Department of Public Safety** 220 E. Bay St., Jacksonville 32202 (Telephone: 904-356-5432).

F66 **CONSUMER FRAUD DIVISION** Metropolitan Dade County Justice Bldg., 1351 N.W. 12th St., Miami 33125 (Telephone: 305-371-7671).

F67 **CONSUMER PROTECTION DIVISION** Dade County, 1351 N.W. 12th St., Miami 33125 (Telephone: 305-377-5111).

F68 **FTC FIELD OFFICE** 931 New Federal Bldg., 51 S.W. First Ave., Miami 33130 (Telephone: 305-350-5540).

F69 **TRADE STANDARDS OFFICE** 1114 Courthouse, Miami 33130.

F70 **DIRECTOR OF CONSUMER AFFAIRS** 264 First Ave., N., St. Petersburg 33701 (Telephone: 813-894-1392).

F71 **ATTORNEY GENERAL OF FLORIDA** State Capitol, Tallahassee 32304 (Telephone: 904-222-3440).

F72 **DIVISION OF CONSUMER SERVICES** Florida Department of Agriculture and Consumer Services, The Capitol, Tallahassee 32304 (Telephone: 904-599-7284).

The Division is a clearinghouse for consumer complaints, and has the responsibility for informing the public about frauds and business schemes through the news media. The Florida Consumers Council was appointed to represent statewide organizations. The Council sponsors consumer legislation and assists with the consumer education program. A series of *Wise Shopper* pamphlets is available on food, clothing, fibers, and household equipment. Other booklets include: *Teen-Ager: Watch Out for Gyps!*; *How to Sue in Small Claims Court*; and *What to Do When You Have Been Cheated*. *The Comparison Shopper* (a cost-per-ounce guide) and a complaint form are also available.

F73 **FLORIDA CONSUMERS ASSOCIATION, INC.** Box 3552, Tallahassee 32303.

PUBLICATIONS:

Florida Small Loan Law and Consumer Finance Law, Regulations. Revised February 8, 1963, affirmed and reissued April 20, 1966. Tallahassee, Comptroller's Office, 1966.

Truth in Lending in Florida. Tallahassee, Florida Bar Association, Continuing Legal Education, 1970.

GEORGIA

F74 **ATTORNEY GENERAL** 132 State Judicial Bldg., Atlanta 30334.

F75 COUNCIL OF STATE GOVERNMENTS, Southern Office 830 W. Peachtree St., N.W., Atlanta 30308.

F76 FDA DISTRICT OFFICE 60 Eighth St., N.E., Atlanta 30309.

F77 FTC FIELD OFFICE Room 720, 730 Peachtree St., N.E., Atlanta 30308 (Telephone: 404-526-5836).

F78 GEORGIA CONSUMER COUNCIL Box 311, Morris Brown College, Atlanta 30314 (Telephone: 404-525-7831, ext. 69).

F79 GEORGIA CONSUMER SERVICES PROGRAM State Department of Family and Children Services, 15 Peachtree St., Atlanta 30303 (Telephone: 404-577-2680).
This Program offers free advice and assistance concerning product buying and money management to less fortunate citizens in Georgia. It helps people to recognize standards of price and quality; to be aware of merchant obligations and consumer rights; to avoid misunderstood contracts; to manage money and budget properly; and to avoid unnecessary debts. One of its services is a statewide WATS line. Georgians can call free, from anywhere in the state, for advice on individual money and buying problems. A catalog of books, pamphlets, posters, films, and tapes is available.

F80 SOUTHEAST REGION PLENTIFUL FOODS PROGRAM Consumer and Marketing Service, USDA, Rm. 206, 1718 Peachtree Rd., N.W., Atlanta 30309 (Telephone: 404-526-3855).

PUBLICATION:
Consumption and Expenditure Analysis for Meat, Meat Products, and Eggs in Atlanta, Georgia. Robert Rausihar, J.C. Purcell, and J.C. Elrod. Athens, Georgia Agricultural Experiment Station, University of Georgia, College of Agriculture, 1965.

HAWAII

F81 ATTORNEY GENERAL Honolulu 96813.

F82 DEPARTMENT OF EDUCATION Office of Instructional Services, State of Hawaii, Honolulu 96813.

A teacher's packet containing materials for consumer education is available.

F83 FTC FIELD OFFICE 508 1st Federal Savings and Loan Bldg., 843 Fort Street Mall, Honolulu 98613 (Telephone: 808-537-9200).

F84 OFFICE OF CONSUMER PROTECTION Office of the Governor, 602 Kamamalu Bldg., 250 S. King St., P.O. Box 3767, Honolulu 96811 (Telephone: 808-531-5995).

This Office was established to protect the interests of both the legitimate businessman and the consumer public. Complaints and requests for information may be referred to the above Office, the Governor's liaison offices, or the following State Department of Social Services offices: 75 Aupuni St., Hilo 96720; State Office Bldg., Main St., P.O. Box 889, Wailuku 96793; State Office Bldg., 3060 Eiwa St., P.O. Box 8, Lihue 96766; P.O. Box 7, Kaunakakai 96748. A Consumer Advisory Council also is available to discuss consumer problems or to suggest improvements for rendering better service to consumers.

PUBLICATIONS:

Consumer Financing Costs and Practices in Hawaii. Edward Wilson Read. Honolulu, Economic Research Center, University of Hawaii, 1960.

Co-signing: law and practices of consumer cash loans and consumer installment credit by lending institutions in Hawaii. Patricia K. Putnam, Honolulu, University of Hawaii, 1963.

IDAHO

F85 ASSISTANT ATTORNEY GENERAL, Consumer Protection

Division State Capitol, Boise 83707 (Telephone: 208-384-2400).

ILLINOIS

F86 **ATTORNEY GENERAL, Consumer Protection Division** Rm. 900, 160 N. LaSalle St., Chicago 60601 (Telephone: 302-793-2500).
This Division was created to combat deceptive and fraudulent business practices and to protect honest businesses from unfair competition. Copies of the Consumer Fraud Act, Retail Installment Sales Act, and Motor Vehicle Retail Installment Sales Act are distributed, as well as a unit pricing guide and general consumer information brochures.

F87 **CHICAGO CONSUMER PROTECTION COMMITTEE** 55 E. Monroe St., Suite 1437, Chicago 60603 (Telephone: 312-353-4423).

F88 **CONSUMER FEDERATION OF ILLINOIS** 5420 South East View Park, Chicago 60615 (Telephone: 312-643-1997).

F89 **COUNCIL OF STATE GOVERNMENTS, Midwestern Office** 1313 E. 60th St., Chicago 60637.

F90 **DEPARTMENT OF CONSUMER SALES AND WEIGHTS AND MEASURES** City Hall, 121 N. LaSalle St., Chicago 60602 (Telephone: 312-744-4091).

F91 **FDA DISTRICT OFFICE** 1222 Post Office Bldg., 433 W. Van Buren St., Chicago 60607.

F92 **FTC FIELD OFFICE** 55 E. Monroe St., Suite 1437, Chicago 60603 (Telephone: 312-353-4423).

F93 **ILLINOIS FEDERATION OF CONSUMERS** 53 W. Jackson Blvd., Chicago 60604.

F94 MIDWEST REGION PLENTIFUL FOODS PROGRAM Consumer and Marketing Service, USDA, Rm. 992, 536 S. Clark St., Chicago 60605 (Telephone: 312-353-6667).

PUBLICATIONS:

Food, Drug, Cosmetic, and Pesticide Laws Study Commission. Report to the Legislature. Chicago, 1967.

Guidelines for Consumer Education. Springfield, Office of the Superintendent of Public Instruction, June 1968.

INDIANA

F95 ATTORNEY GENERAL OF INDIANA 219 State House, Indianapolis 46204 (Telephone: 317-633-5512).

F96 CONSUMER ADVISORY COUNCIL Indiana Department of Commerce, 336 State House, Indianapolis 46204 (Telephone: 317-633-4228).

F97 CONSUMERS ASSOCIATION OF INDIANA, INC. 910 N. Delaware St., Indianapolis 46402 (Telephone: 317-634-7396).

F98 COOPERATIVE EXTENSION SERVICE Purdue University, Lafayette 47906.

PUBLICATION:

Health Regulations and the Indiana Food Industry. John S. Waggaman. Bloomington, Institute of Public Administration, Indiana University, 1965.

IOWA

F99 COOPERATIVE EXTENSION SERVICE Iowa State University, Ames 50010.

Materials offered include: *Working Wives; Automation in Our Lives; Community Volunteers; Cashing in on Cars; Speak*

Up, Consumers!; *Your Family Business Affairs*; and *Consumer Marketing Bulletin*.

F100 **VISUAL INSTRUCTION SERVICE** 121 Pearson Hall, Iowa State University, Ames 50010.
A 25-slide presentation, "Law and Labels," is available.

F101 **CONSUMER EDUCATION AND PROTECTIVE OR-GANIZATION** 1016 University Ave., Des Moines 50311.

F102 **CONSUMER PROTECTION DIVISION** Iowa Department of Justice, 220 E. 13th Court, Des Moines 50319 (Telephone: 515-281-5926).
This Division enforces the Consumer Protection Laws, handles complaints from consumers, and drafts and recommends bills to the Legislature. A publication, *Consumer Protection at the State Level*, 1971, discusses the state's consumer protection acts, its consumer education programs, and the general need for consumer protection.

F103 **IOWA CONSUMERS LEAGUE** P.O. Box 1076, Des Moines 50311 (Telephone: 515-279-3644).

KANSAS

F104 **COOPERATIVE EXTENSION SERVICE** Kansas State University, Manhattan 66502.
Materials offered include: *Your Future Is Now*; *A Look at You the Consumer*; *Consumer Rights and Responsibilities*; *Be a Wide Awake Consumer*; *Consumer Information Series to Help Select Major Appliances*; and *Fabrics and Their Care*.

F105 **DEPARTMENT OF FAMILY ECONOMICS** Justin Hall, Kansas State University, Manhattan 66502.
Of interest are *Effect of DOD Directive No. 1344.7 on Creditors Bordering Fort Riley*, and *Consumer Program for Kansas*, a 20-point consumer quiz.

F106 KANSAS CITY CONSUMERS ASSOCIATION 7720 W. 61st St., Shawnee Mission 66202.

F107 CONSUMER PROTECTION DIVISION Office of the Attorney General, State Capitol Bldg., Topeka 66612 (Telephone: 913-296-2215).

The Division protects Kansas consumers from certain illegal and fraudulent business practices and carries out the duties of the Buyers' Protection Act.

F108 CONSUMER PROTECTION DIVISION Sedgwick County Courthouse, Wichita 67203 (Telephone: 316-268-7405).

A booklet, *Help Yourself! A Handbook on Consumer Frauds*, describes some common frauds, how to avoid them, and what to do if deceived. It includes a directory of agencies at the local, state, and national levels and their areas of consumer interests.

PUBLICATION:

Kansas Consumer Loan Act, and Rules and Regulations, Kansas Sales Finance. Topeka, Office of Consumer Credit Commissioner, 1965.

KENTUCKY

F109 ASSISTANT ATTORNEY GENERAL, Consumer Protection Division State Capitol, Frankfort 40601 (Telephone: 502-564-4513).

F110 CITIZENS' COMMISSION FOR CONSUMER PROTECTION State Capitol, Frankfort 40601 (Telephone: 502-564-6607).

F111 COOPERATIVE EXTENSION SERVICE University of Kentucky, Lexington 40506.

Materials offered include: *Buyers Guide for Household Equipment*; *Guides to Better Shopping*; *Guarantees and Warranties*; *Bare Facts About Labeling*; *Gimmicks in the Marketplace*; and *Refund—Exchange—Complaint*.

F112 COUNCIL OF STATE GOVERNMENTS, Headquarters Iron Works Pike, Lexington 40505.

F113 CONSUMER ASSOCIATION OF KENTUCKY, INC. 706 E. Broadway, Louisville 40202.

F114 DIVISION OF WEIGHTS AND MEASURES AND CONSUMER AFFAIRS 2nd Fl., Metropolitan Sewer District Bldg., Louisville 40202 (Telephone: 502-582-2206).

F115 COOPERATIVE EXTENSION SERVICE Eastern Kentucky University, Richmond 40475.

Materials available include: *Guide for Teaching Lower Income Consumers*; *The Consumer is King*; and *Flip Charts on Credit*.

PUBLICATIONS:

Kentucky Narcotic, Barbiturate, and Amphetamine Drug Laws and Regulations. Frankfort, Kentucky State Department of Health, Office of Investigation and Narcotic Control, 1965.

Report of the Condition of Licensed Consumer Loan Companies. Frankfort, Department of Banking.

LOUISIANA

F116 ATTORNEY GENERAL The Capitol, Baton Rouge 70804.

F117 LOUISIANA CONSUMERS' LEAGUE P.O. Box 1332, Baton Rouge 70821 (Telephone: 504-926-3738).

F118 FDA DISTRICT OFFICE 222 U.S. Customhouse, 423 Canal St., New Orleans 70130.

F119 FTC FIELD OFFICE 1000 Masonic Temple Bldg., 333 St. Charles St., New Orleans 70130 (Telephone: 504-527-2091).

F120 NEW ORLEANS CONSUMER PROTECTION COMMIT-TEE 1000 Masonic Temple Bldg., 333 St. Charles St., New Orleans 70130 (Telephone: 504-527-2041).

F121 TOTAL COMMUNITY ACTION, INC. 615 North St., New Orleans 70130 (Telephone: 504-581-4301).

MAINE

F122 ASSISTANT ATTORNEY GENERAL, Consumer Protection Division State House, Augusta 04330 (Telephone: 207-289-3661).

MARYLAND

F123 MARYLAND CONSUMERS ASSOCIATION, INC. P.O. Box 143, Annapolis 21404 (Telephone: 301-268-3331).

F124 CONSUMER PROTECTION DIVISION Office of the Attorney General, 12th Fl., One S. Calvert St., Baltimore 21202 (Telephone: 301-539-5413).
This Division handles consumer complaints concerning deceptive or dishonest sales techniques and issues leaflets alerting the consumer to these problems. There are seven consumer advisory offices in addition to the Baltimore office: City Hall, Cumberland; Court House, Easton; JAG Office, Fort Meade; Court House, Hagerstown; Court House, Salisbury; County Service Building, Silver Spring; and Court House, Upper Marlboro.

F125 FDA DISTRICT OFFICE 900 Madison Ave., Baltimore 21201.

F126 LEGAL AID BUREAU, INC. 341 N. Calvert St., Baltimore 21202 (Telephone: 301-539-5340).
In addition to regular services, the Bureau offers information

on protection from dishonest door-to-door salesmen. Other legal aid offices located in Baltimore are: 622 Aisquith St. 21202 (Telephone: 301-675-5218); 1803 Pennsylvania Ave. 21217 (Telephone: 301-669-5695); 710 Cherry Hill Rd. 21225 (Telephone: 301-354-1120); and 1435 W. Baltimore St. 21223 (Telephone: 301-945-6040).

F127 **CONSUMER PROTECTION DIVISION**   Prince Georges County Court House, Upper Marlboro 20870 (Telephone: 301-627-3000).

MASSACHUSETTS

F128 **BOSTON METROPOLITAN CONSUMER PROTECTION COMMITTEE**   JFK Federal Bldg., Government Center, Boston 02203.

F129 **CONSUMER PROTECTION DIVISION**   Department of the Attorney General, State House, Boston 02133 (Telephone: 617-727-5520).
   The Division enforces Massachusetts laws protecting consumers from fraud, deceptive advertising and sales practices, and violation of credit laws; investigates complaints; takes legal action to enforce consumer protection laws; develops consumer protection legislation; and prepares consumer information materials. A form to be used for registering complaints is provided. Illustrated *Consumer Information Leaflets* covering timely consumer problems include a brief description of protective laws and information that should be noted by the consumer.

F130 **CONSUMER'S COUNCIL**   Commonwealth of Massachusetts, 100 Cambridge St., Boston 02202 (Telephone: 617-727-2605).
   The Council was established as a statutory body in 1963 to act "as the people's advocate in the governmental structure as well as the marketplace"; to coordinate consumer services and further consumer education; to keep the public informed on

consumer issues; to conduct studies concerning consumer problems and initiate consumer legislation; and to advise the Governor and the General Court on matters concerning the consumers' interest. It publishes a monthly *Consumers' Council News* summarizing legislative programs, activities of the Council, and items of general interest to the consumer.

F131 **FDA DISTRICT OFFICE** 585 Commercial St., Boston 02109.

F132 **FTC FIELD OFFICE** JFK Federal Bldg., Government Center, Boston 02203 (Telephone: 617-223-6621).

F133 **MASSACHUSETTS CONSUMER ASSOCIATION** 27 School St., Boston 02108.

F134 **BOSTON CONSUMERS' COUNCIL** 218 Weld Ave., West Roxbury 02119 (Telephone: 617-323-5291).

PUBLICATION:
Narcotic and Harmful Drug Laws. Boston, Department of Public Health, Division of Food and Drugs, 1968.

MICHIGAN

F135 **BUREAU OF REGULATION** Department of Licensing and Regulation, 200 Lafayette Bldg., Detroit 48226.
This Bureau investigates consumer complaints against residential builders and residential maintenance and alteration contractors and salesmen.

F136 **CONSUMER ALLIANCE OF MICHIGAN** c/o Michigan Credit Union League, P.O. Box 5210, Detroit 48235 (Telephone: 313-341-9074).

F137 **CONSUMER RESEARCH ADVISORY COUNCIL** 16596 Normandy, Detroit 48221.

F138 FDA DISTRICT OFFICE 1560 E. Jefferson Ave., Detroit 48207.

F139 INTRAGENCY CONSUMER COMMISSION Office of the Mayor, City Hall, Detroit 48226 (Telephone: 313-224-3440).

F140 MICHIGAN STATE UNIVERSITY College of Human Ecology, Department of Human Environment and Design, East Lansing 48823.

The Consumer Seminar Series was initiated in the spring of 1970 in an effort to bridge communication gaps between consumers and industry. Representatives from manufacturers, retailers, government, and the university participate in this exchange of ideas and solutions to the consumer/industry communications problem.

F141 SAFETY AND ENFORCEMENT DIVISION Michigan Department of State, 1331 E. Grand River, East Lansing 48823.

This Division investigates complaints lodged against vehicle dealers.

F142 GREAT SCOTT! SUPER MARKETS, INC. 1111 E. Eight Mile Rd., Ferndale 48220 (Telephone: 313-564-6100).

Through the cooperation of this food chain and Cass Methodist Church, once a week residents of Detroit's inner city are bused to a suburban supermarket, where prices are lower than in the city.

F143 DETROIT CONSUMERS ASSOCIATION 29207 Ford Rd., Garden City 48135.

F144 CONSUMER PROTECTION DIVISION Department of the Attorney General, Law Bldg., Lansing 48902 (Telephone: 517-373-1152).

The Division endeavors to mobilize resources of law enforcement agencies, business organizations, service clubs, labor organizations, and public and private clubs in the war against consumer frauds. It initiates legislation, brings criminal actions against individuals and organizations, and engages in educational programs.

F145 DETROIT CONSUMER PROTECTION COORDINATING COMMITTEE Law Bldg., Lansing 48902 (Telephone: 517-373-1110).

F146 FINANCIAL INSTITUTIONS BUREAU Michigan Chamber of Commerce, Seven Story Office Bldg., 525 W. Ottawa St., Lansing 48913.

This Bureau supervises the operation of state-chartered banks, trust companies, credit unions, savings and loan associations, and small loan companies and regulates the issuance and sale of money orders.

F147 FOOD INSPECTION DIVISION Michigan Department of Agriculture, Fifth Fl., Lewis Cass Bldg., Lansing 48913.

This Division has the authority to inspect the sanitary conditions in all food handling establishments; to check labels and all types of advertising media; to require proper labeling and packaging; to remove from trade channels misbranded, adulterated, decomposed, and putrid foods or foods containing illegal additives, chemicals, spray residues, preservatives, or supplements; to test the accuracy of commercial weighing and measuring devices; to prevent the sale of any commodity or service fraudulently represented; to enforce legal standards for food products; and to investigate consumer complaints in connection with reported violations of any food or weights and measures laws.

F148 MICHIGAN CONSUMER COUNCIL 525 Hollister Bldg., Lansing 48933 (Telephone: 517-373-0947).

F149 POLICYHOLDERS SERVICE UNIT Insurance Bureau, Michigan Department of Commerce, 111 N. Hosmer St., Lansing 48912.

The Bureau regulates the insurance business in Michigan; the Policyholders Service Unit assists the public in settling disputes with insurance companies concerning such things as claims, premium payments, and cancellations.

F150 SECURITIES BUREAU Michigan Department of Commerce, Seven Story Bldg., 525 W. Ottawa St., Lansing 48913.
This Bureau polices the operators of debt management businesses.

F151 SPECIAL ASSISTANT TO THE GOVERNOR FOR CONSUMER AFFAIRS 1033 S. Washington St., Lansing 48910 (Telephone: 517-373-1870).

PUBLICATION:
Abstract of Reports of Small Loan Licensees. Lansing, State Banking Department.

MINNESOTA

F152 FDA DISTRICT OFFICE 240 Hennepin Ave., Minneapolis 55401.

F153 MINNESOTA CONSUMERS LEAGUE 1671 S. Victoria Rd., St. Paul 55118 (Telephone: 612-221-6732).

F154 OFFICE OF CONSUMER SERVICES Department of Commerce, 230 State Office Bldg., St. Paul 55101 (Telephone: 612-221-2162).

F155 SPECIAL ASSISTANT ATTORNEY GENERAL FOR CONSUMER PROTECTION 102 State Capitol, St. Paul 55101 (Telephone: 612-221-3854).

PUBLICATIONS:
Dairy and Food Laws, St. Paul.
Report of Small Loan Companies. St. Paul, Banking Division.

MISSISSIPPI

F156 MISSISSIPPI CONSUMER ASSOCIATION 1601 Terrace Rd., Cleveland 38732 (Telephone: 601-843-5731 or 601-843-8883).

F157 ASSISTANT ATTORNEY GENERAL IN CHARGE OF CONSUMER PROTECTION State Capitol, Jackson 39201 (Telephone: 601-354-7134).

F158 CONSUMER PROTECTION DIVISION Department of Agriculture and Commerce, Jackson 39205 (Telephone: 601-354-6586).

MISSOURI

F159 CITIZENS CONSUMER ADVISORY COMMITTEE 7701 Forsyth Blvd., Clayton 63104 (Telephone: 314-863-4654).

F160 MISSOURI ASSOCIATION OF CONSUMERS P.O. Box 514, Columbia 65201 (Telephone: 314-449-9331 or 314-442-5329).

The purposes of the Association are to gather, exchange, and disseminate information on matters of interest to consumers; to promote consumer education; and to assist and coordinate the efforts of other consumer groups.

F161 ATTORNEY GENERAL, Consumer Protection Division Box 899, Jefferson City 65101 (Telephone: 314-636-7131).

The Division issues two leaflets, *It Can Happen to You* (consumer protection advice for older citizens) and *Are You Making a Large Purchase* (consumer protection advice on contract signing). Both give the addresses and telephone numbers of three consumer protection offices to which problems and questions may be addressed.

F162 FDA DISTRICT OFFICE 1009 Cherry St., Kansas City 64106.

F163 KANSAS CITY CONSUMER ASSOCIATION 940 S. Woodland Dr., Kansas City 64118.

F164 FTC FIELD OFFICE Rm. 1302, 208 North Broadway, St. Louis 63102 (Telephone: 314-622-4710).

F165 ST. LOUIS CONSUMER FEDERATION 6321 Darlow Dr., St. Louis 62123 (Telephone: 314-638-3859).
The Federation acts as a communication between consumers and government and advocates a direct-action approach to consumer problems. Its education program consists of public meetings, workshops on current legislative consumer problems, a nutrition and buying course, demonstrations on grading and labeling, and movies. As part of this education program, the *Bulletin* is issued periodically, covering activities of the Federation and local, state, and federal developments in areas of consumer interest.

MONTANA

F166 MONTANA CONSUMER AFFAIRS COUNCIL P.O. Box 2447, Great Falls 59401.

F167 ATTORNEY GENERAL The Capitol, Helena 59601.

NEBRASKA

F168 ATTORNEY GENERAL The Capitol, Lincoln 68509.

PUBLICATION:
Consolidated Annual Reports Filed by Small Loan Companies. Lincoln, Small Loan Division.

NEVADA

F169 CONSUMER PROTECTION AGENCY Nevada Commerce Department, Nye Bldg., Carson City 89701 (Telephone: 702-882-7366).

NEW HAMPSHIRE

F170 ATTORNEY GENERAL OF NEW HAMPSHIRE State House Annex, Concord 03301 (Telephone: 603-271-3641).

NEW JERSEY

F171 CAMDEN COUNTY OFFICE OF CONSUMER AFFAIRS 606 Commerce Bldg., One Broadway, Camden 08101 (Telephone: 609-964-8700).

F172 CONSUMERS LEAGUE OF NEW JERSEY 20 Church St., Montclair 07042 (Telephone: 201-744-6449).

The League is a voluntary organization founded in 1900 to protect consumers in the marketplace and to promote consumer responsibility for the conditions under which goods are produced and distributed. It gathers facts, analyzes issues, and makes the information available to the public and lawmakers; serves as a clearinghouse for exchange of consumer information among other groups; conducts a legislative program; organizes statewide conferences and legislative forums on consumer protection, migratory farm labor, and health needs; receives consumer complaints and refers them to governmental agencies for investigation, if requested to do so; provides information on current legislation and events; and issues a bimonthly *Newsletter* and a weekly press column, "For the Consumer."

F173 DIVISION OF CONSUMER AFFAIRS Department of Law and Public Safety, State of New Jersey, 1100 Raymond Blvd., Newark 07102 (Telephone: 201-648-3622).

This Division has the responsibilities of: advising the Governor and the Attorney General on matters affecting the public as consumers and recommending legislation it deems necessary;

appearing before governmental agencies in behalf of consumer interests; and assisting in the coordination of federal, state, and municipal activities relating to consumer affairs, as well as cooperating with other consumer organizations. The Citizens Consumer Affairs Advisory Committee consults with and advises the Division on programs, policy, and research to meet consumer needs. Several pamphlets are available in English and Spanish.

F174 OFFICE OF CONSUMER PROTECTION Attorney General of New Jersey, 1100 Raymond Blvd., Newark 07102 (Telephone: 201-648-2012).

PUBLICATION:
Legal Representation of the Poor; A Guide for New Jersey's Legal Services Project Attorneys. Edited by Eli Jarmal, Director, Institute for Continuing Legal Education. Newark, 1968.

NEW MEXICO

F175 ALBUQUERQUE CONSUMERS ASSOCIATION 4844 Southern Ave., S.E., Albuquerque 87108 (Telephone: 505-277-3114).

F176 COOPERATIVE EXTENSION SERVICE New Mexico State University, Las Cruces 88001.

F177 CONSUMER PROTECTION DIVISION Office of the Attorney General, Department of Justice, P.O. Box 2246, Santa Fe 87501 (Telephone: 505-827-5237).
The Division is concerned with the enforcement of laws protecting consumers from unlawful, unfair, fraudulent, or deceptive business practices and/or advertising. It creates programs for public information and solicits participation of organized community and industry groups in exposing and combating fraudulent and misleading schemes. The Division publishes and distributes a brochure, *20 Ways Not to be Gypped.*

NEW YORK

F178 FDA DISTRICT OFFICE Rm. 700, 850 Third Ave. at 30th St., Brooklyn 11232.

F179 FDA DISTRICT OFFICE 599 Delaware Ave., Buffalo 14202.

F180 DEPARTMENT OF WEIGHTS AND MEASURES AND OFFICE OF CONSUMER AFFAIRS County of Orange, Goshen 10924 (Telephone: 914-294-5822).

F181 COOPERATIVE EXTENSION SERVICE College of Human Ecology, Cornell University, Ithaca 14850.
A total program of educational supplements includes "Textile Seminar to Train Singer Employees," "Textiles for Retailers," and "Household Refuse: Its Potential for Reduction and Reuse."

F182 CORNELL UNIVERSITY Mailing Room, Bldg. 7, Research Park, Ithaca 14850.
"Be a Better Shopper" is a 100-slide presentation, including a leader's guide, set of "Better Shopper Record Sheets," a cost-weight table, and *Be a Better Shopper Bulletin.*

F183 CONSUMER AFFAIRS City Hall, Long Beach 11561 (Telephone: 516-421-1000).

F184 OFFICE OF CONSUMER AFFAIRS County of Nassau, 160 Old Country Rd., Mineola 11501 (Telephone: 516-535-3282).
The first consumer affairs office in the nation to be created at the county level, the Nassau group receives and investigates complaints and initiates investigations of frauds and unfair practices against consumers; conducts consumer education and information programs; cooperates with local, state, and federal agencies to protect and promote interests of consumers; encourages local business and industry to maintain high standards of honesty and fair business practices; and operates a mobile

field unit to reach low-income consumers with programs for their protection, information, and education. Many publications, films, and slides are available, including *Consumer's Guide to Government and Private Agencies.*

F185 CONSUMER ASSEMBLY OF GREATER NEW YORK, INC. 40 United Housing Foundation, 465 Grand St., New York 10002.

F186 CONSUMER FRAUDS AND PROTECTION BUREAU Department of Law, State of New York, 368 State Office Bldg., 80 Centre St., New York 10013 (Telephone: 212-488-4304).

The Bureau protects consumers in New York State through six areas of activity: mediation; education; litigation; legislation; industry and business orientations; and governmental, quasi-governmental, and nongovernmental assistance. Pamphlets illustrating specific frauds are distributed in both English and Spanish. Complaints are handled by the Bureau and by the New York State Attorney General's offices at the following locations: The Capitol, Albany; Metcalf Bldg., Auburn; Press Bldg., Binghamton; 65 Court St., Buffalo; 48 Cornelia St., Plattsburgh; 2 Catharine St., Poughkeepsie; 65 Broad St., Rochester; and 339 E. Washington St., Syracuse.

F187 CONSUMER PROTECTION BOARD 380 Madison Ave., New York 10017 (Telephone: 212-488-5320).

F188 COUNCIL OF STATE GOVERNMENTS, Eastern Office 36 W. 44th St., New York 10036.

F189 DEPARTMENT OF CONSUMER AFFAIRS 80 Lafayette St., New York 10013 (Telephone: 212-964-7777).

This municipal agency performs the following services: investigates and resolves consumer complaints, sponsors and supports consumer legislation, tests purchases and checks commodities offered for sale, inspects regularly all weighing and measuring devices in commercial use, investigates false and misleading advertising, licenses over 100 businesses and occupations, and enforces Department regulations for licensed operations. Weekly food price surveys also are conducted. Timely consumer information is available by calling Consumerfone, 964-2525. Two booklets offered are *How to Sue in Small Claims Court in New York City* and *Where to Go*, a directory outlining services available from city, state, federal, and private agencies.

F190 **FEDERAL RESERVE BANK OF NEW YORK** 33 Liberty St., New York 10045.
This bank offers *The Story of Checks*.

F191 **FIRST NATIONAL CITY BANK** 55 Wall St., New York 10005.
This bank offers *Know Your Money*, a brochure prepared for bank associates, and *Consumer Views*, a newsletter.

F192 **FTC FIELD OFFICE** 22nd Fl., Federal Bldg., 26 Federal Plaza, New York 10007 (Telephone: 212-264-1200).

F193 **METROPOLITAN NEW YORK CONSUMER COUNCIL** 1710 Broadway, New York 10019 (Telephone: 212-673-3900).

F194 **NORTHEAST REGION PLENTIFUL FOODS PROGRAM** Consumer and Marketing Service, USDA, Rm. 1645, 26 Federal Plaza, New York 10007 (Telephone: 212-264-4642).

F195 **CONSUMER ASSOCIATION OF NEW YORK** 101 Heather Dr., Rochester 14625 (Telephone: 716-381-5958).

F196 **CONSUMER COUNCIL OF MONROE COUNTY** Rochester Institute of Technology, Metropolitan Center, 50 Main St., W., Rochester 14614 (Telephone: 716-325-4000, ext. 30).

PUBLICATIONS:
Consumer Education. Albany, Bureau of Continuing Education, Curriculum Development, 1969.
Consumer Education for High Schools. New York, New York City Board of Education, Bureau of Curriculum Development, 1969.

Consumer Education in Lincoln High School, A Case Study. Lincoln High School, Yonkers. Mt. Vernon, Consumers Union, 1965.

Consumer Education: Materials for an Elective Course. Albany, The University of the State of New York, State Education Department, Bureau of Secondary Curriculum Development, 1967.

NORTH CAROLINA

F197 FTC FIELD OFFICE Rm. 206, 623 E. Trade St., Charlotte 28202 (Telephone: 704-333-6762).

F198 AMERICAN CONSUMER CORPORATION P.O. Box 4294, Fayetteville 28306 (Telephone: 919-425-7331).

F199 CONSUMER SERVICES UNLIMITED (CSU) P.O. Box 5831, Fayetteville 28303 (Telephone: 919-488-9201).
CSU offers its members discounts on merchandise from local merchants and maintains a consumer advisory board. A monthly newsletter summarizes current government activities in the consumer area.

F200 AGRICULTURAL EXTENSION SERVICE School of Agriculture and Life Sciences, North Carolina State University, Raleigh 27607.
There are 101 County Extension Offices located throughout North Carolina.

F201 BANKING DEPARTMENT State of North Carolina, Raleigh 27602 (Telephone: 919-829-3016).
The Banking Department supervises state chartered banks, loan companies, the sale of checks (money order companies), and preburial contracts acquired by funeral homes. Complaints or inquiries dealing with the above may be directed to the Banking Department.

F202 CONSUMER PROTECTION DIVISION Department of

Justice, State of North Carolina, P.O. Box 629, Raleigh 27602.
This Division has the duty to investigate alleged breaches of, and enforce, laws relating to fraud and deception in commerce; to investigate alleged breaches of, and enforce, laws relating to antitrust matters; to represent the interests of the general consuming public at hearings before all state and federal administrative agencies; and to provide legal advice, counsel, and representation to specified state agencies.

F203 **NORTH CAROLINA BANKERS ASSOCIATION** Bankers-Insurance Bldg., Raleigh 27601 (Telephone: 919-833-6481).
Member banks act as clearinghouses for citizen communication to North Carolina senators and representatives in the U.S. Congress. Forms to be used for complaints or inquiries are supplied by the banks. The completed forms are then forwarded to North Carolina congressmen in Washington.

F204 **NORTH CAROLINA CONSUMER FINANCE ASSOCIATION, INC. (NCCFA)** 603 Raleigh Bldg., Raleigh 27601 (Telephone: 919-833-2859).
NCCFA is the official trade association representing the majority of state licensed and supervised consumer loan and finance companies in North Carolina. Through its educational programs, NCCFA attempts to provide to the public information on the basic principles of consumer credit and personal financial planning. Affiliated with the National Consumer Finance Association, NCCFA offers a teacher's kit on consumer credit and a catalog of educational materials.

F205 **NORTH CAROLINA CONSUMER COUNCIL, INC.** P.O. Box 10273, Raleigh 27605 (Telephone: 919-834-3529).

F206 **NORTH CAROLINA MILK COMMISSION** 11 S. Boylan Ave., Raleigh 27603 (Telephone: 919-829-3733).
The North Carolina Legislature assigned to the Commission the task of maintaining a stable milk industry from the dairy farm to the consumer. It does so by setting and enforcing fair

trade practice rules. It publishes *Questions and Answers About Milk* and the *North Carolina Dairy Report*.

F207 WAKE INFORMATION CENTER Wake County Public Library Headquarters, 104 Fayetteville St., Raleigh 27601 (Telephone: 919-833-1132).

This community service offered by the Wake County Public Library system refers residents to the local office, agency, department, or person that can help with problems. *Help for the Citizens of Wake County* is a 92-page directory designed to assist neighborhood leaders and the man on the street to find out where to go for help. Problems, needs, and services are listed alphabetically. An index to 300 agencies and organizations and a section on Wake County civic groups are also included.

PUBLICATION:

Some Aspects of Consumer Credit in North Carolina with Special Reference to South Carolina and Virginia. William Hays Simpson (Durham) in cooperation with College of General Studies, University of South Carolina, Columbia, 1970.

NORTH DAKOTA

F208 OFFICE OF ATTORNEY GENERAL Bismarck 58501 (Telephone: 701-224-2217).

The state's consumer fraud law gives the Attorney General's Office the authority to bring action in a District Court of the state to enjoin any practice declared unlawful by this law. The Office accepts complaints and investigates such complaints. Once it is determined that a violation of the consumer fraud law is evident, the Attorney General's Office will institute legal proceedings on behalf of the state and, when citizens have been victimized by an unlawful act, will request the Court to grant an order restoring to such persons any amounts they have paid as a result of such unlawful act.

F209 BISMARCK-MANDAN CONSUMERS LEAGUE 1105 Sunset Dr., Mandan 58544.

OHIO

F210 CONSUMER CONFERENCE OF GREATER CINCINNATI 318 Terrace Ave., Cincinnati 45220 (Telephone: 513-861-4288).

F211 FDA DISTRICT OFFICE 1141 Central Pkwy., Cincinnati 45202.

F212 CONSUMER PROTECTION ASSOCIATION 118 St. Clair Ave., Cleveland 44114 (Telephone: 216-241-0186).

F213 CONSUMERS LEAGUE OF OHIO 940 Engineers Bldg., Cleveland 44114 (Telephone: 216-621-1175).
The League's program is based on investigation, education, and legislation concerning consumer problems, as well as air and water pollution and pesticides.

F214 FTC FIELD OFFICE 1339 Federal Office Bldg., 1240 E. 9th St., Cleveland 44199 (Telephone: 216-522-4207).

F215 CITY SEALER OF WEIGHTS AND MEASURES City Hall, Columbus 43215 (Telephone: 614-461-7397).

F216 CONSUMER FRAUDS AND CRIMES SECTION Office of the Attorney General, Columbus 43215 (Telephone: 614-469-4986).
This Section operates as a clearinghouse for consumer complaints and a public information agency for consumer frauds and crimes. The Office of the Attorney General publishes a *Newsletter*, often of direct concern to consumers, and a *Consumer Frauds and Crimes Bulletin*.

F217 HOME ECONOMICS EDUCATION Vocational Education Division, State Department of Education, Columbus 43215.
Among the materials offered are: *Curriculum Guide; Consumer Education—Curriculum Guide for Ohio, Grades K-12;* and *Home Economics Supplement in Consumer Education Curriculum Guide for Ohio, Grades K-12.*

F218 **OHIO CONSUMERS ASSOCIATION**   P.O. Box 1559, Columbus 43216 (Telephone: 614-228-4711, ext. 8463).

Among its activities are consumer education, coordination of consumer efforts, work to establish a consumer voice in government, study and promotion of consumer legislation, and research on consumer problems.

OKLAHOMA

F219 **DEPARTMENT OF CONSUMER AFFAIRS**   74 Lincoln Office Plaza, 4545 Lincoln Blvd., Oklahoma City 73105 (Telephone: 405-521-3653).

F220 **CONSUMERS COUNCIL OF OKLAHOMA, INC.**   240 E. Apache, Tulsa 74106 (Telephone: 918-584-0001).

OREGON

F221 **COOPERATIVE EXTENSION SERVICE**   Oregon State University, Corvallis 97331.

Among the materials available are: *The Truth-in-Lending Law and Your Credit*; *Credit Cards—30 Days to Reality*; *Use Your Consumer Credit Wisely*; and *Spotlight,* a newsletter on food marketing information.

F222 **FTC FIELD OFFICE**   231 U.S. Courthouse, Portland 97205 (Telephone: 503-226-3361).

F223 **METROPOLITAN CONSUMER PROTECTION AGENCY**   Multnomah County Court House, Portland 97204 (Telephone: 503-224-8840).

F224 **OREGON CONSUMER LEAGUE**   3110 N.W. Luray Terr., Portland 97210 (Telephone: 503-228-8787).

F225 **ASSISTANT ATTORNEY GENERAL FOR ANTITRUST AND CONSUMER PROTECTION** Attorney General of Oregon, 322 State Office Bldg., Salem 97310 (Telephone: 503-378-4733).

F226 **ASSISTANT TO THE GOVERNOR FOR ECONOMIC DEVELOPMENT AND CONSUMER SERVICES** State Capitol Bldg., Salem 97301 (Telephone: 503-378-3015).

PUBLICATIONS:

Oregon's Agriculture and Food Statutes, 1963. Salem, State Department of Agriculture, 1964.

Summary of Reports Filed by Consumer Finance Licensees and Industrial Loan Companies. Banking Division.

PENNSYLVANIA

F227 **PENNSYLVANIA LEAGUE FOR CONSUMER PROTECTION** P.O. Box 948, Harrisburg 17108 (Telephone: 717-233-5704).

F228 **CONSUMERS EDUCATION AND PROTECTIVE ASSOCIATION (CEPA)** 6048 Ogontz Ave., Philadelphia 19141 (Telephone: 215-424-1441).

CEPA is a nonprofit, unincorporated association organized for mutual education and protection of low-income consumers. There are seven branches in Philadelphia and four in surrounding communities. Consumers present complaints or grievances at weekly branch meetings. Volunteer committees check the complaints, contact the companies involved, send delegations to negotiate settlements, and, when necessary, engage in picketing and distributing leaflets. CEPA publishes a 4-page monthly newspaper, *Consumers Voice.* A paperback manual, *The Living History of CEPA, 1966–1968,* is a useful guide in organizing groups.

F229 CONSUMER SERVICES Rm. 210, City Hall, Philadelphia 19106 (Telephone: 215-686-2797).

F230 FDA DISTRICT OFFICE 1204 U.S. Customhouse, Second and Chestnut Sts., Philadelphia 19106.

F231 PHILADELPHIA AREA CONSUMER ORGANIZATION 1320 W. Hunting Park Ave., Philadelphia 19140.

F232 ALLEGHENY COUNTY BUREAU OF CONSUMER PROTECTION 209 Jones Law Bldg. Annex, Pittsburgh 15219 (Telephone: 412-355-5402).

F233 BUREAU OF CONSUMER PROTECTION Department of Justice, 1405 State Office Bldg., Pittsburgh (Telephone: 412-565-5135).

The Bureau has five offices in Pennsylvania to which the consumer may address requests for information or complaints: Durbin Bldg., 204 North Market Sq., Harrisburg 17101 (Telephone: 717-787-7109); 711 State Office Bldg., Philadelphia 19130 (Telephone: 215-568-4000, ext. 7001); 402 Connell Bldg., 129 N. Washington Ave., Scranton 18503 (Telephone: 717-346-8435); 815½ State St., Erie 16501 (Telephone: 814-454-7184); and the above Pittsburgh office. The Bureau issues brochures on timely consumer problems, explaining legal protection available, ways to avoid mistakes, where to register complaints, and specific problems of the aged. A "Budget Gadget" is available which provides the consumer with a guide to prices per ounce, costs of meats and eggs, grades of beef, can sizes, grade labeling, egg quality, and approximate number of servings per pound of meat.

F234 COOPERATIVE EXTENSION SERVICE The Pennsylvania State University, University Park 16802.

Materials available include *Tools for Teaching the Budget-Minded Shopper* and miscellaneous consumer releases.

F235 FTC FIELD OFFICE 53 Long La., Upper Darby 19082 (Telephone: 215-352-9365).

F236 PHILADELPHIA CONSUMER PROTECTION COMMITTEE 53 Long La., Upper Darby 19082 (Telephone: 215-352-9365).

PUBLICATION:

The Consumer Finance Industry in Pennsylvania. Randall Stuart Stout, Bureau of Business Research, College of Business Administration, Pennsylvania State University. University Park, 1963.

RHODE ISLAND

F237 RHODE ISLAND CONSUMERS LEAGUE 2 Progress Ave., East Providence 02914.

F238 RHODE ISLAND CONSUMER'S COUNCIL State of Rhode Island, 365 Broadway, Providence 02902 (Telephone: 401-277-2764).

The Council is organized into the Division of Consumer Affairs and the Division of Consumer Credit Counseling. The Division of Consumer Affairs handles complaint mediation; education and information; education projects; legislation; studies; surveys; research and analyses; and fraud, deception, and misrepresentation. The Division of Consumer Credit Counseling offers advice to families and individuals on money management or developing a debt payment plan and sponsors educational programs designed to teach consumers how to avoid spending themselves into bankruptcy.

F239 SPECIAL ASSISTANT ATTORNEY GENERAL Providence County Court House, Providence 02903 (Telephone: 401-831-6850).

SOUTH CAROLINA

F240 ATTORNEY GENERAL Hampton Office Bldg., Columbia 29201.

PUBLICATION:
The Operation of All Loan Agencies in South Carolina; a Report to the 94th Legislature of South Carolina by the Committee Created by Joint Resolution No. 893 of the 1960 Acts and Joint Resolutions. Columbia,Committee to Investigate the Operation of All Loan Agencies, 1961.

SOUTH DAKOTA

F241 SOUTH DAKOTA CONSUMERS LEAGUE P.O. Box 106, Madison 57402.

F242 OFFICE OF CONSUMER AFFAIRS Attorney General of South Dakota, State Capitol, Pierre 57501 (Telephone: 605-224-3215).

PUBLICATION:
Study of the South Dakota State Food and Drug Laws. Staff Background Memorandum. Pierre, State Legislative Research Council, 1966.

TENNESSEE

F243 ATTORNEY GENERAL Supreme Court Bldg., Nashville 37219.

F244 TENNESSEE ADVISORY COMMISSION ON CONSUMER PROTECTION State of Tennessee, Nashville 37219.

F245 TENNESSEE CONSUMER ALLIANCE, INC. P.O. Box 12352, Acklen Sta., Nashville 37212 (Telephone: 615-741-2991).

F246 FTC FIELD OFFICE G-209 Federal Office Bldg., P.O. Box 568, Oak Ridge 37830 (Telephone: 615-483-8611).

TEXAS

F247 ANTITRUST AND CONSUMER PROTECTION DIVISION Attorney General of Texas, Capitol Sta., P.O. Box 12548, Austin 78711 (Telephone: 512-475-3288).

F248 OFFICE OF CONSUMER CREDIT 1011 San Jacinto Blvd., P.O. Box 2107, Austin 78767 (Telephone: 512-475-2111).

F249 TEXAS AGRICULTURAL EXTENSION SERVICE Texas A&M University, College Station 77840.
Materials prepared for a consumer education workshop are available.

F250 FDA DISTRICT OFFICE 3032 Bryan St., Dallas 75204.

F251 FTC FIELD OFFICE 405 Thomas Bldg., 1314 Wood St., Dallas 75202 (Telephone: 214-749-3057).

F252 SOUTHWEST REGION PLENTIFUL FOODS PROGRAM Consumer and Marketing Service, USDA, Rm. 5C32, 1100 Commerce St., Dallas 75202 (Telephone: 214-749-3273).

F253 TEXAS CONSUMER ASSOCIATION Suite 99, 505 N. Ervoy Bldg., Dallas 75201.

F254 FTC FIELD OFFICE 10511 U.S. Courthouse Bldg., 515 Rusk Ave., Houston 77061 (Telephone: 713-226-4738).

F255 FTC FIELD OFFICE 417 U.S. Post Office and Courthouse, 615 Houston St., San Antonio 78206 (Telephone: 512-225-5511).

PUBLICATIONS:

Institute on Texas Regulatory Loan Act, 1963; the Model Act for the Regulation of Credit Life Insurance and Credit Accident and Health Insurance, September 5–7, 1963. Albert P. Jones, Chairman, Institute on Texas Regulatory Loan Act. Austin, University of Texas, 1963.

Texas Food, Drug and Cosmetic Laws.   Austin, Texas State
Department of Health, 1963.
The Small Loan Industry in Texas.   Donald A. Tyree. Aus-
tin, Bureau of Business Research, University of Texas, 1960.
Research Memorandum 19.

UTAH

F256   COOPERATIVE   EXTENSION   SERVICE   Utah   State
University, Logan 84321.
Materials available are *Consumer Alert* and *Market News.*

F257   ADMINISTRATOR OF CONSUMER CREDIT   403 State
Capitol, Salt Lake City 84114 (Telephone: 801-328-5461).

F258   ASSISTANT ATTORNEY GENERAL FOR CONSUMER
PROTECTION   State Capitol, Salt Lake City 84114 (Telephone: 801-328-5261).

F259   LEAGUE   OF   UTAH   CONSUMERS   c/o   Utah   Credit
Union League, 1706 Major St., Salt Lake City 84115.

VERMONT

F260   CONSUMER INFORMATION CLEARINGHOUSE   Cooperative Extension Service, Terrill Hall, University of Vermont, Burlington 05401.
The Clearinghouse provides consumer information and education, prepares legislation, serves as a referral agency, and offers
suggestions as to suitable lines of action in consumers' problems.
It works closely with the state's Consumer Protection Bureau.
Dollars and Decisions is a bimonthly publication of the Clearinghouse. It also has a weekly news column in all daily and
weekly publications within the state; a weekly radio tape for
all radio stations in the state and adjacent areas; two monthly
television programs on consumer protection; and a monthly

"consumer hot line," hour-long feature on educational television, with phoned-in questions to be answered by a panel of experts. *They're Out to Sell You* . . . flyers cover specific consumer problems. *Where Do I Find Out About* . . . flyers give names and addresses of groups or agencies that handle specific complaints. *Vermont Farm and Home Publications* lists popular and technical publications. *A Pocket Guide for Consumers* is also available.

F261 **CONSUMER PROTECTION BUREAU** Attorney General of Vermont, 94 Church St., Burlington 05401 (Telephone: 802-864-0111).

F262 **FAMILY ECONOMICS AND HOME MANAGEMENT SPECIALIST** 210 Terrill Hall, University of Vermont, Burlington 05401 (Telephone: 802-656-3280).

F263 **VERMONT CONSUMERS' ASSOCIATION** 72 Lakewood Pkwy., Burlington 05401.

VIRGINIA

F264 **VIRGINIA CITIZENS CONSUMER COUNCIL** P.O. Box 3103, Alexandria 22302 (Telephone: 703-836-4388).

The Council began in 1966 by focusing its concern on rising prices. Its interests have extended to misleading advertisements, shoddy goods and services, and, through committees, it has launched a number of local action programs. The Council provides speakers upon request and publishes a bimonthly newsletter. It sponsors a complaint service and provides testimony before legislative bodies, encouraging strong consumer protection measures. A consumer message is recorded weekly and may be heard by dialing 549-4220 at any time.

F265 **FTC FIELD OFFICE, Washington, D.C. Area** 450 W. Broad St., Falls Church 22046 (Telephone: 703-533-3243).

F266 **PENINSULA CONSUMER LEAGUE, INC.** 648 Bellwood Rd., Newport News 23605.

F267 **ATTORNEY GENERAL OF VIRGINIA** Supreme Court, Library Bldg., Richmond 23219 (Telephone: 703-770-2071).

F268 **OFFICE OF CONSUMER AFFAIRS** Departments of Agriculture and Commerce, P.O. Box 1163, Richmond 23209 (Telephone: 703-770-2042).
  This Office receives complaints on alleged illegal, fraudulent, deceptive, or dangerous practices from Virginia consumers and refers such complaints to the state and local departments or agencies charged with enforcement of consumer laws, to Better Business Bureaus, and to associations.

F269 **SPECIAL ASSISTANT TO THE GOVERNOR ON MINORITY GROUPS AND CONSUMER AFFAIRS** Office of the Governor, Richmond 23219 (Telephone: 703-770-2211).

F270 **CONSUMER PROTECTION OFFICER** Bureau of Consumer Protection, Inspections Division, City Hall, Virginia Beach 23456 (Telephone: 703-427-4421).

WASHINGTON

F271 **CONSUMER PROTECTION DIVISION** Office of the Attorney General, Temple of Justice, Olympia 98501 (Telephone: 206-464-7744).
  This Division attempts to alert the consumer to common problems, ways to avoid problems, laws to protect the consumer, and agencies that can be of assistance. Branches of the Consumer Protection Division are located at Dexter Horton Bldg., Seattle 98104; Old National Bank Bldg., Spokane 99200; and 1502 Tacoma Ave., Tacoma 98402.

F272 **DEPARTMENT OF AGRICULTURE** General Administration Bldg., Olympia 98501.

F273 **DEPARTMENT OF MOTOR VEHICLES** Highways-Licenses Bldg., Olympia 98501.

F274 **INSURANCE COMMISSIONER** Insurance Bldg., Olympia 98501.

F275 **REAL ESTATE DIVISION** Department of Motor Vehicles, Highways-Licenses Bldg., Olympia 98501.

F276 **SECURITIES DIVISION, In-State Firms** Department of Motor Vehicles, Olympia 98501.

F277 **UTILITIES AND TRANSPORTATION COMMISSION** Highways-Licenses Bldg., Olympia 98501.

F278 **FDA DISTRICT OFFICE** 501 Federal Office Bldg., 909 First Ave., Seattle 98104.
A recorded consumer message may be heard in the Seattle area by dialing 583-0108.

F279 **FTC FIELD OFFICE** 908 Republic Bldg., 1511 Third Ave., Seattle 98101 (Telephone: 206-583-4655).

F280 **INTERSTATE COMMERCE COMMISSION** 6130 Arcade Bldg., 1319 Second Ave., Seattle 98101.

F281 **SECURITIES AND EXCHANGE COMMISSION, Interstate** Hoge Bldg., Seattle 98104.

F282 **WAGE & CLAIM DIVISION** Department of Labor and Industries, 1601 Second Ave., Seattle 98104.

F283 **WASHINGTON COMMITTEE ON CONSUMER INTERESTS** 815 36th Ave., E., Seattle 98102 (Telephone: 206-324-8611).

F284 **BETTER BUSINESS BUREAUS** Denny Bldg., Seattle 98121 (622-8066); Columbia Bldg., Spokane 99204 (747-1155); Rust Bldg., Tacoma 98402 (383-5561); and 103 N. Third, Yakima 98901 (453-6529).

These Bureaus provide information on reliability of firms or individuals in business.

F285 CONSUMER CREDIT COUNSELING 2402 Third Ave., Seattle 98121 (622-3290); West 521 Maxwell, Spokane 99201 (326-2140); and 2220 Sixth Ave., Tacoma 98403 (383-3826).

This group provides nonprofit credit advice and assistance at minimal charge.

F286 LAWYER REFERRAL SERVICE 605 Arctic Bldg., Seattle 98104 (623-1443); 1020 Paulsen Bldg., Spokane 99201 (747-8658); and Pierce County Legal Assistance, 1501 S. M St., Tacoma 98405 (383-4804).

This Service provides assistance in obtaining legal advice at minimal charge.

F287 LEGAL SERVICES 1401 S. Jackson St., Seattle 98144 (324-7477); West 318 Sprague Ave., Spokane 99201 (747-4118); and 1501 S. M St., Tacoma 98405 (383-4804).

These offices offer free legal service for persons with low income.

WEST VIRGINIA

F288 ATTORNEY GENERAL OF WEST VIRGINIA The Capitol, Charleston 25305 (Telephone: 304-348-3377).

F289 CONSUMER PROTECTION DIVISION West Virginia Department of Labor, 1900 Washington St., East Charleston 25305 (Telephone: 304-348-2195).

F290 CONSUMER ASSOCIATION OF WEST VIRGINIA 410 12th Ave., Huntington 25701 (Telephone: 304-523-4558).

F291 COOPERATIVE EXTENSION SERVICE Appalachian Center, West Virginia University, Morgantown 26505.
What's in Your Shopping Bag is available.

PUBLICATION:

Retail Credit Policies in West Virginia. Edwin W. Crooks. Morgantown, Bureau of Business Research, College of Commerce, West Virginia University, 1965.

WISCONSIN

F292 BUREAU OF CONSUMER PROTECTION Department of Agriculture, 801 W. Badger Rd., Madison 53713 (Telephone: 608-266-7228).

F293 CONSUMER AFFAIRS COORDINATOR Attorney General of Wisconsin, Department of Justice, Madison 53702 (Telephone: 608-266-7340).

F294 WISCONSIN CONSUMERS LEAGUE P.O. Box 1531, Madison 53701.

The League is a statewide, voluntary, nonprofit, nonpartisan organization established to provide service and protection through information, education, and action. It publishes the *Newsletter* for its members.

F295 THE GREATER MILWAUKEE CONSUMER LEAGUE 9722 Watertown Plank Rd., Milwaukee 53226 (Telephone: 414-258-8740).

PUBLICATION:

Wisconsin Administrative Code; Rules of State Department of Agriculture. Madison, State Department of Agriculture, 1964.

WYOMING

F296 STATE EXAMINER AND ADMINISTRATOR Consumer Credit Code, State Supreme Court Bldg., Cheyenne 82001 (Telephone: 307-777-7797).

Local: Government and Private

In previous Directories, specific consumer groups have been mentioned. However, sometimes the need for assistance is urgent, and there is no time to call or write a group outside the area. There are many local sources that should be able to advise on problems and to provide needed information quickly. Local laws and statutes, city ordinances, and codes offer protection for the consumer. The people and organizations listed below should be useful resources.

City and County Government Offices

Mayor's Office
City Manager
City Council
District Attorney
County Attorney
Police Department
Health Department
Small Claims Court
Family Services and Child Welfare

Public Defender
Adult Education Programs
Public Libraries
Offices of Weights, Measures, and Markets
County Agricultural Extension Service Agents
Board of Education
Welfare Agencies

Community Programs and Services

Chamber of Commerce
Better Business Bureau
YMCA and YWCA
Neighborhood Houses
Churches and Religious Groups
Settlements
Salvation Army
Legal Aid Society
League of Women Voters
Labor Unions
Newspapers
Banks, Credit Unions, and Savings & Loan Associations

Medical and Dental Societies
Bar Association
Lawyers Referral Service
Poison Control Centers
Hospitals
Real Estate Boards
Retail Associations
Cooperatives
Colleges and Universities
Community Consumer Organizations
Education Associations

State Government Offices at Local Level

Department of Education
State Insurance Commissioner

Senators and Congressmen

Federal Government Offices at Local Level

U.S. Postal Inspector

Senators and Congressmen

National Nongovernment

This Directory includes private associations, businesses, manufacturers, and groups operating nationally, but not affiliated with the government. Some of the groups were formed solely for the purpose of aiding the consumer, while others have included an area of consumer information or education as a service to the public. A few of the organizations listed are voluntary; the majority are private, profit or nonprofit organizations. Some are research-oriented; others are civic-minded; and still others are professional and trade associations. Again, the information listed was received from the groups named.

H1　ACME MARKETS, INC.　124 N. 15th St., Philadelphia, Pa. 19102.
　　This food chain has instituted unit pricing and open dating. Its *Freshness Guide* explains the coding program and is available to all Acme customers.

H2　AEROSOL EDUCATION BUREAU　300 E. 44th St., New York, N.Y. 10017 (Telephone: 212-661-3721).
　　The Bureau offers *Will Death Come Without Warning?*— a pamphlet warning of the dangers of deliberate abuse of aerosols.

H3　ALA AUTO AND TRAVEL CLUB　1047 Commonwealth Ave., Boston, Mass. 02215.

H4 **AMERICAN ASSOCIATION OF UNIVERSITY WOMEN (AAUW)** 2401 Virginia Ave., N.W., Washington, D.C. 20037.

Of interest in the *AAUW Publication List* are materials in the legislative and community action categories.

H5 **AMERICAN BANKERS ASSOCIATION** 90 Park Ave., New York, N.Y. 10016 (Telephone: 212-972-5100).

The Association offers a booklet, *Personal Money Management,* and an educational film package on personal money management and savings (including a 16-mm color motion picture film, filmstrip, teacher's guide, and student practice materials).

H6 **AMERICAN BAR ASSOCIATION (ABA)** 1155 E. 60th St., Chicago, Ill. 60637 (Telephone: 312-493-0533).

The ABA offers *Your Home Buyer's Guide*—a 14-page pamphlet outlining steps to follow and pitfalls to avoid when purchasing a home.

H7 **AMERICAN COUNCIL ON CONSUMER INTERESTS (ACCI)** 238 Stanley Hall, University of Missouri-Columbia, Columbia, Mo. 65201.

ACCI is an organization of professionals in consumer affairs and education. It serves these professionals by keeping them up-to-date on the latest developments in the consumer field and promotes an exchange of ideas among the members. Publications include: *The Journal of Consumer Affairs; The ACCI Newsletter; Consumer Education Forum;* a consumer directory; and proceedings from annual conferences.

H8 **AMERICAN FEDERATION OF LABOR AND CONGRESS OF INDUSTRIAL ORGANIZATIONS** Department of Community Services, 815 16th St., N.W., Washington, D.C. 20006 (Telephone: 202-293-5000).

One program of the Department of Community Services is Consumer Counselling, aimed at informing and educating union members on consumer problems. The three parts of this program are the consumer information course, the consumer conference, and the consumer clinic. Several publications in support of union action at the community level are available: *Consumer Counselling, Debt Counselling, Course Outlines for Information Classes,* and *Consumer Counselling, Education, Information for the Poor.*

H9 AMERICAN HOME ECONOMICS ASSOCIATION 2010 Massachusetts Ave., N.W., Washington, D.C. 20036 (Telephone: 202-833-3100).

The Association strives—through its subject matter and professional sections and committees—to improve the quality and standards of individual and family life through education, research, cooperative programs, and public information. Its publications include a number of items of interest to the consumer in areas of family economics and home management, food and nutrition, textiles and clothing, and health and welfare. These include: *Consumer Education—Opportunity and Challenge; Consumer Credit in Family Financial Management; Answers to Questions Consumers Ask About Meat and Poultry;* and *Consumer Color Chart.*

H10 AMERICAN HOTEL AND MOTEL ASSOCIATION 888 Seventh Ave., New York, N.Y. 10019.

H11 AMERICAN MEDICAL ASSOCIATION 535 N. Dearborn St., Chicago, Ill., 60610.

The Association issues pamphlets such as *Health Quackery, Mechanical Quackery,* and *The Merchants of Menace* to alert customers to the misleading advertising and ineffectiveness of many health products and special remedies.

H12 AMERICAN NATIONAL STANDARDS INSTITUTE (ANSI) 1430 Broadway, New York, N.Y. 10018.

A federation of trade, technical, labor, and consumer organizations, companies, and government agencies, the Institute acts as a clearinghouse to coordinate the work of standards development in the private sector. The Consumer Council is an administrative arm of ANSI, assuring that consumer interests are represented in the development and approval of voluntary national standards. A catalog of standards, such as specifications for accident prevention tags, is available.

H13 AMERICAN PETROLEUM INSTITUTE 1801 K St., N.W., Washington, D.C. 20006.

The Institute offers *Know Your Motor Oil; The Can People;* and *Recycling and the Can in the Seventies.*

H14 AMTRAK, NATIONAL RAILROAD PASSENGER COR-PORATION Director of Public Affairs, 955 L'Enfant Plaza, Washington, D.C. 20024.

H15 ARMOUR AND COMPANY Consumer Service Department, P.O. Box 9222, Chicago, Ill. 60600.

Armour makes available its *Meat Guide.*

H16 ASSOCIATED CREDIT BUREAUS, INC. (ACB) 6767 Southwest Freeway, Houston, Tex. 77036.

The ACB is an international trade association serving the credit bureau industry. It is the responsibility of local credit bureaus to help consumers maintain their credit records; to identify—to credit granters—consumers who are qualified to receive credit; and to assist consumers when they encounter credit difficulty.

H17 ASSOCIATION FILMS, INC. 600 Madison Ave., New York, N.Y. 10022.

Offers three films in its consumer series: "Our Role as Consumers," "Consumers in the Market Place," and "Consumers in Action." "Consumer Education in the Nation's Schools" is a survey of 5,000 home economists.

H18 BUDGET GADGET P.O. Box 38161, Los Angeles, Calif. 90038 (Telephone: 213-788-7693).

The "Budget Gadget" (see Figure 6), available to individuals and organizations, is a device for comparing prices of different size eggs, packages and cans, and cuts of meat. It has been distributed by the State of Pennsylvania's Department of Justice as part of its consumer education program and by the Kansas Home Economics Association, the Kansas Food Dealers Association, and the Santa Barbara Savings and Loan Association. Prices range from $0.50 each for 1 to 4 copies to $0.15 each for 2,500 to 5,000 copies; other quantity prices are available from H. Morris at the above address.

Figure 6. The Budget Gadget helps the shopper compare prices and sizes to buy the most economical item.

H19 CENTER FOR CONSUMER AFFAIRS University Extension, University of Wisconsin, 600 W. Kilbourn Ave., Milwaukee, Wis. 53203.

The Center conducts studies, conferences, workshops, and meetings on major consumer problems. A newsletter provides ongoing information on consumer and environmental issues such as packaging, detergents, recycling, utilities, and transportation.

H20 CHAMBER OF COMMERCE OF THE UNITED STATES, Consumer Affairs Committee 1615 H St., N.W., Washington, D.C. 20006 (Telephone: 202-659-6120).

The Committee is composed of over 50 business, trade association, and local Chamber executives and works toward the implementation of programs in the consumer issues area. The Council on Trends and Perspectives identifies significant economic, social, technological, and political changes and anticipates their effects. Its studies have included *Business and the Consumer—A Program for the Seventies.* The National Economic Development Group prepares analyses of legislative proposals pending before Congress, often represented by charts such as the ones shown in Figure 7, and testifies on consumer affairs before congressional committees. Though directed primarily to business, the Chamber's publications and activities are of interest to consumers. *Let's Revitalize Business-Consumer Relations* provides a program guide for local Chambers. *Consumer Conference Guides* on food, clothing, appliances, and credit are for the use of local Chambers working to maintain good relationships between consumers and business. "The Consumer Revolution" is a 15-minute slide presentation for businessmen that describes the challenge of the consumer revolution to business and offers tips for meeting it.

H21 CHANGING TIMES EDUCATION SERVICE 1729 H St., N.W., Washington, D.C. 20006.

The Service offers a monthly teachers journal; resource kit on earning, spending, borrowing, budgeting, and saving; mini units

Prepared in the National Economic Development Group
Chamber of Commerce of the United States
Washington, D.C. 20006

January 10, 1973

For additional information, contact:
Nancy Nord   (202) 659-6127
Lawrence B. Kraus   (202) 659-6126

COMPARISON OF MAJOR CONSUMER REPRESENTATION BILLS
PENDING IN THE HOUSE

Subject	H.R. 14 (Rosenthal)	H.R. 564 (Fuqua)	H.R. 21 (Hollifield)
1. Structure	Would create a statutory Office of Consumer Affairs in the Executive Office of the President and an independent Consumer Protection Agency within the Executive Branch. It would also create a Consumer Advisory Council.	Would create an independent Consumer Protection Agency within the Executive Branch.	Would create a statutory Office of Consumer Affairs in the Executive Office of the President and an independent Consumer Protection Agency within the Executive Branch.
2. Purposes	The Office of Consumer Affairs would coordinate Federal consumer activities and generally promote consumer interests. The Consumer Protection Agency would act as advocate of consumer interests in agency and court proceedings. The Consumer Advisory Council would advise the Agency and Office on matters relating to consumer interests.	The Consumer Protection Agency would represent the interests of consumers before Federal agencies and courts, receive and transmit consumer complaints, and develop and disseminate information of interest to consumers.	The Office of Consumer Affairs would coordinate Federal consumer activities and promote consumer interests generally. The Consumer Protection Agency would act as advocate of consumer interests in agency and court proceedings

Figure 7. Comparison of Major Consumer Representation Bills Pending in the House.

on cars, environment, jobs, money management, credit, business and economics, and clothing and personal; and a games booklet including role playing and the complaint game.

H22 CHEMICAL SPECIALTIES MANUFACTURERS ASSO-CIATION 50 E. 41st St., New York, N.Y. 10017.

The Association membership represents all facets of the chemical specialties industry. Its six divisions are: aerosol; automotive; detergents and cleaning compounds; disinfectants and sanitizers; insecticides; and waxes, polishes, and floor finishes. As part of its effort to ensure safe and effective use of household chemical products, the Association publishes and distributes *Your Child and Household Safety*.

H23 COMMERCE CLEARING HOUSE, INC. (CCH) 4025 W. Peterson Ave., Chicago, Ill. 61646.

CCH offers to business and industry federal and state laws, rules, regulations, orders, and decisions—in looseleaf form—which are updated on a regular basis. Among the topics included are *Consumerism; Food, Drug, Cosmetic Law Reports; Consumer Credit Guide and Secured Transactions Guide; Insurance Law Reports;* and *Medicare-Medicaid Guide.* Also available are *Congressional Index*, teaching aids, books, school texts, and periodicals.

H24 CONSUMER BANKERS ASSOCIATION (CBA) 840 Washington Bldg., 1725 K St., N.W., Washington, D.C. 20006 (Telephone: 202-393-0491).

Although an association of banks, CBA provides information to the consumer on installment lending and other consumer banking activities.

H25 CONSUMER FEDERATION OF AMERICA (CFA) Suite 1105, 1012 14th St., N.W., Washington, D.C. 20005 (Telephone: 202-737-3732).

Organized for and dedicated to consumer action through legislation, information, and education, CFA is a federation of national, state, regional, and community consumer organizations.

It encourages the creation of such groups; provides services to work cooperatively with other consumer groups; stimulates and coordinates consumer programs in areas such as product pricing, product quality, servicing, guarantees, regulatory agencies, credit and insurance, home improvements, cost of food, drugs and medical care, and safety; serves as a clearinghouse for the exchange of information, ideas, and experiences among members at the city, county, regional, state, and national levels; provides a responsible and articulate voice for consumers by gathering facts, analyzing consumer issues, and making this information available to the public and to lawmakers; stimulates and provides consumer information and education; maintains continuing liaison with members of Congress and decision makers in federal departments and agencies; prepares legislative fact sheets; prepares and presents testimony on consumer issues; coordinates legislative activities of consumer organizations; and sponsors the annual Consumer Assembly in Washington, D.C. A selected bibliography of consumer books is available.

H26   CONSUMER PRODUCT INFORMATION Washington, D.C. 20407.

H27   CONSUMER RESEARCH ADVISORY COUNCIL 3127 E. Canfield, Detroit, Mich. 48207 (Telephone: 313-571-6700).

The Council was organized in 1966 to assist low-income consumers in their purchase of goods and services. Its Consumer Coordinating Centers supplement the services of other agencies to fulfill the need for specific information and expertise in meeting everyday needs of people in the communities which they serve. Information on a variety of consumer subjects, geared to the requests and needs of consumers, is available. The Council publishes *The Consumer Guardian.*

H28   CONSUMER RESEARCH INSTITUTE, INC. (CRI) Suite 300, 1632 K St., N.W., Washington, D.C. 20006 (Telephone: 202-628-4927).

CRI sponsors and/or conducts research in the areas of industry marketing practices and their relationships to consumer concerns. Although primarily concerned with research about consumer attitudes and behavior, it has undertaken projects concerned with consumer information needs, new product evaluation, and government operations in consumer protection.

H29   CONSUMERS' RESEARCH, INC. Washington, N.J. 07882.
Established in the 1920s, Consumers' Research conducts scientific and engineering tests of products that consumers buy and use. Based on the results of these tests, it rates the products as A – Recommended, B – Intermediate, and C – Not Recommended. Its findings are published in the *Consumer Bulletin* and the *Consumer Bulletin Annual*. Four series of color slides and lectures are also available: "Testing at Consumers' Research," "Deceptive Packaging," "Food Additives," and "Safety in the Home."

H30   CONSUMERS UNION OF THE UNITED STATES, INC. (CU) 256 Washington St., Mount Vernon, N.Y. 10050.
Consumers Union is the world's largest consumer testing and information organization. Its monthly publication, *Consumer Reports*, gives background information on tested products, the significance of CU's findings for the consumer, features to look for in buying, and ratings of either "acceptable" or "not acceptable." The Union also publishes yearly buying guides and participates in government hearings and consumer-oriented conferences. Four of CU's special reports are on life insurance, health products, consumer thinking, and wines and spirits.

H31   COOPERATIVE LEAGUE OF THE USA 59 E. Van Buren St., Chicago, Ill. 60605 (Telephone: 312-922-0726).
The Cooperative League is a federation of national, regional, state, and local organizations—including cooperatives, credit unions, mutual insurance companies, and group health associations—acting together to obtain a great variety of goods and services. Pamphlets, periodicals, films, and filmstrips on cooperatives and how to form them are available. The Washington, D.C. office is located at 1012 14th St., N.W., 20005 (Telephone: 202-628-9000).

H32 COUNCIL FOR FAMILY FINANCIAL EDUCATION 1619 Twin Towers, 1110 Fidler La., Silver Spring, Md. 20910 (Telephone: 301-588-9026).

The Council is an independent, nonprofit, educational corporation to assist schools, colleges, and other institutions in the development and implementation of programs in consumer education as a vital aspect of a national instructional need. It sponsors graduate teacher education programs and in-service training programs in consumer education and makes a listing of these programs available. It has published *Teaching Consumer Education and Financial Planning*; *Family Financial Education for Adults*; *Free and Inexpensive Material*—a selective bibliography of books, publications, films, and filmstrips for teaching consumer education and financial planning; "Budget or Bust"—a two-act play for high schools; "Be Sure! Insure!"—a radio broadcast or assembly program; and "Let the Green-Back Crusader Help"—a 15-minute radio script or playlet for grade seven.

H33 COUNCIL OF BETTER BUSINESS BUREAUS 1150 17th St., N.W., Washington, D.C. 20036.

The Better Business Bureaus are dedicated to building public confidence in the business system. They are fact-finding organizations that investigate and act on complaints of unfair and unethical business practices, promote fair advertising and selling practices, prosecute frauds, and conduct educational programs. The Bureaus issue a fact booklet series on various business subjects and circulate them to individual consumers and employees. A consumer's buying guide, *How to Get Your Money's Worth*, has also been published.

H34 CREDIT UNION NATIONAL ASSOCIATION, INC. (CUNA) Box 431, 1617 Sherman Ave., Madison, Wis. 53701.

CUNA is an international association serving credit union leagues. As part of its consumer information and educational programs, it publishes *Everybody's Money*—a quarterly consumer-oriented publication; *Consumer Facts*—leaflets on various subjects; "Using Your Money"—a consumer education film; and a leaflet explaining credit unions. These items can be obtained by writing to the above address. There is also a Washington, D.C. office located at 1730 Rhode Island Ave., N.W., 20036 (Telephone: 202-659-2360).

H35 DIRECT MAIL ADVERTISING ASSOCIATION 230 Park Ave., New York, N.Y. 10017.

Dissatisfied customers of mail order companies may complain to the Association. The Association will try to obtain satisfaction from the company involved.

H36 DOW JONES & COMPANY, INC. 30 Broad St., New York, N.Y. 10004 (Telephone: 212-422-3115).

This company offers *The Complete Consumer*, *The Consumer's Handbook*, and a list of free materials available to secondary school instructors.

H37 EVAPORATED MILK ASSOCIATION 910 17th St., N.W., Washington, D.C. 20006.

Learning from Labels is available from this group.

H38 FEDERATION OF HOMEMAKERS 927 N. Stuart St., Arlington, Va. 22203 (Telephone: 703-536-5793).

This voluntary organization is concerned with better protection from food additives. It prepares testimony for, and participates in, Food and Drug Administration hearings and represents its members at hearings on bills pending before the U.S. House and Senate. It publishes a newsletter for its members, plus special-interest pamphlets.

H39 FOLLETT EDUCATIONAL CORPORATION Educational Opportunities Division, 1010 W. Washington Blvd., Chicago, Ill. 60607.

In the *Accent/Consumer Education Series*, these booklets are available: *The Land for You; Social Insurance; Investing Your Savings; Insure Your Life, Income and Property; Containers—*

How to Compare the Prices of Their Contents; and *Understanding Consumer Credit*. Available in the *Family Finance Series* are *On Your Own*; *Head of Household*; and *Family of Five*.

H40 GENERAL MILLS, INC. Betty Crocker Department No. 360, 400 Second Ave., S., Minneapolis, Minn. 55440.

"The How and Why of Packaging" is a film presentation on packaging and labeling for junior and senior high school students. The kit, available on a loan basis, contains a 15-minute, 68-frame, color filmstrip, narration guide, and 25 student booklets.

H41 GENERAL MOTORS CORPORATION General Motors Bldg., 3044 W. Grand Blvd., Detroit, Mich. 48202.

This automobile manufacturer suggests a three-step procedure for customers with questions or complaints: communicate first with the dealer, next with the zone office, and finally with a divisional owner-relations department. GM offers many educational aids, as well as a 19-page booklet, *How to Harvest Abandoned Cars*. All are available from the public relations office at the above address.

H42 GIANT FOOD INC. P.O. Box 1804, Washington, D.C. 20013 (Telephone: 202-341-4711).

Unit pricing, open dating, and nutritional labeling have been instituted by this food chain. Efforts are also directed toward care labeling of fabrics, product safety, and steps to clean up the environment. *Giant Tips to Save $$$$$ in Your Supermarket* and weekly recipe flyers are available. The company's consumer advisor invites customers to write them about their ideas.

H43 GOOD FOOD PEOPLE 165 W. Harvey St., Philadelphia, Pa. 19144.

H44 GRAND UNION COMPANY East Paterson, N.J. 07407.

Grand Union provides consumer information on price-per-measure and code dating in its stores. Pamphlets are available on *Compare-A-Price* and *Freshness Codes*. The latter also includes home care tips for perishable foods.

H45 GROLIER EDUCATIONAL CORPORATION 845 Third Ave., New York, N.Y. 10022.

"Modern Consumer Education"—a multimedia teaching unit —includes 39 lessons, 13 audio cassettes, 27 programmed-learning texts, and 2 filmstrips on food, clothing, shelter, cars, furniture and appliances, protecting family health and security, you and the law, ways to handle money, and ways to shop. It is available at a cost of $200.

H46 HOTPOINT Appliance Park, Louisville, Ky. 40224.
Use and Care Guide—Range is available.

H47 HOOVER HOME INSTITUTE Hoover Company, North Canton, Ohio 44700.
Information on carpets and rugs is available.

H48 HOUSEHOLD FINANCE CORPORATION Money Management Institute, Prudential Plaza, Chicago, Ill. 60601.
Booklets available are *It's Your Credit, Manage It Wisely; Your Guide for Teaching Money Management;* and *Money Management, Your Food Dollar.* "Be Credit Wise" and "Spending Your Food Dollars" are filmstrips.

H49 HUMBLE OIL P.O. Box 2180, Houston, Tex. 77001.
Humble offers *Plain Talk About Our New Efficiency Gasolines.*

H50 HUNT-WESSON KITCHENS Box 3331, Fullerton, Calif. 92634.
Offers three booklets on meal planning and preparation: *The Facts and the Basic 4; The Facts and the Basic Budget;* and *The Facts and the Basic Techniques.*

H51 INSTITUTE OF LIFE INSURANCE 277 Park Ave., New York, N.Y. 10017.
A Date With Your Future is available.

H52 INTERNATIONAL CONSUMER CREDIT ASSOCIA-
TION (ICCA)   375 Jackson Ave., St. Louis, Mo. 63130 (Telephone: 314-727-4045).
ICCA is a not-for-profit membership corporation that provides informational, educational, and association services to
members engaged in some phase of consumer credit service.
Among the publications available is *How to Use Consumer
Credit Wisely*, which gives facts about installment purchasing,
charge accounts, service credit, and personal loans.

H53 JOINT COMMISSION ON ACCREDITATION OF HOS-
PITALS (JCAH)   645 N. Michigan Ave., Chicago, Ill. 60611
(Telephone: 312-642-6061).
This voluntary organization surveys hospitals and other
health-care institutions and facilities and evaluates them in relation to well-defined and accepted sets of standards. The voluntary accreditation service is provided to hospitals upon their
request and at their expense. JCAH will consider complaints
when a hospital is up for re-accreditation. A list of current
publications is available.

H54 JOINT COUNCIL ON ECONOMIC EDUCATION   1212
Avenue of the Americas, New York, N.Y. 10036.
A 109-frame, color cartoon—"The Role of Consumers"—is
available.

H55 KROEHLER MANUFACTURING COMPANY   Consumer
Education Division, Naperville, Ill. 60540.
This company offers a home furnishings classroom kit, as well
as three *Let's Talk About* booklets: *Furniture Quality and Construction*; *Furniture Styling*; and *Upholstery Fabrics*.

H56 KROGER CO.   1014 Vine St., Cincinnati, Ohio 45201.
Kroger food stores have tested unit pricing of groceries and
open dating of perishable products. In its effort to disseminate
information on nutrition to consumers, the company has prepared *The Kroger Basic 4 Cookbook*.

H57 MAJOR APPLIANCE CONSUMER ACTION PANEL 20 N. Wacker Dr., Chicago, Ill. 60606.

H58 MAN-MADE FIBER PRODUCERS ASSOCIATION, INC. 350 Fifth Ave., New York, N.Y. 10001 (Telephone: 212-563-4671).

Educational materials available include: *Man-Made Fiber Fact Book*; *Guide to Man-Made Fibers*; and *Man-Made Fibers*. The *Fact Book* also lists educational materials available from fiber producers.

H59 MANUFACTURING CHEMISTS ASSOCIATION (MCA) 1825 Connecticut Ave., N.W., Washington, D.C. 20009.

MCA is a nonprofit trade association that provides a channel through which member companies can deal with such industry-wide matters as safety, transportation, environmental health, education, and public and government relations. Its Consumer Information Office publishes booklets and leaflets on food additives, pollution, and the chemical industry and distributes slides and filmstrips on food additives. *The Chemical Industry Helps Education* describes various teaching aids.

H60 RALPH NADER Washington, D.C.

At this writing, Attorney Ralph Nader has organized five groups to investigate and report on various areas of consumer dissatisfaction.

Aviation Consumer Action Project (ACAP) P.O. Box 19029, Washington, D.C. 20036.

ACAP's purpose is to provide an effective voice for environmental and consumer concerns regarding aviation. Among its objectives are reductions in air fares, maximum air safety, better service, and consumer representation at regulatory proceedings and before Congress.

Center for Auto Safety National Press Bldg., Washington, D.C. 20004 (Telephone: 202-638-0420).

Through studies of mail complaints on auto safety, the Center identifies trends in occurrence of defects and brings the data to the attention of the National Highway Safety Bureau. In some instances, the Center files suit.

The Center for Study of Responsive Law   P.O. Box 19367, Washington, D.C. 20036 (Telephone: 202-833-3400).

This group is concerned with investigating activities of Federal Government agencies and with publishing reports of these investigations.

Project on Corporate Responsibility   2008 Hillyer Place, N.W., Washington, D.C. 20015 (Telephone: 202-387-8655).

This Project is attempting to provide consumers and shareholders with a voice in policy-making decisions of corporations.

Public Interest Research Group   Suite 601, 1025 15th St., N.W., Washington, D.C. 20005 (Telephone: 202-833-9700).

This group of lawyers studies problems such as tax assessments, mobilizes community action to file suits in such areas as air pollution, petitions government organizations for actions in favor of citizens' interests, and files suit against organizations when appropriate. The Group has sponsored a "Conference on Computers and Consumer Choice," a public discussion of the need for computerized information retrieval systems that would provide information to aid consumers in making decisions.

The following reports have been prepared by these groups on their investigations:

The Nader Report on the Federal Trade Commission.   By Edward F. Cox and Robert Fellmeth. New York, R.W. Baron, 1969. $5.95.

The Interstate Commerce Commission.   By Robert Fellmeth. New York, Grossman, 1970. $8.95.

Vanishing Air.   Edited by John C. Esposito. New York, Grossman, 1970. $6.95; paperback $0.95.

The Chemical Feast.   Edited by James S. Turner. New York, Grossman, 1970. $6.95; paperback, $0.95.

One Life—One Physician: An Inquiry Into the Medical Pro-

fession's Performance in Self-Regulation. Edited by Robert S. McCleery, M.D. Washington, D.C., Public Affairs Press, 1970. $5.

Old-Age: The Last Segregation. By Claire Townsend, Project Director. New York, Grossman, 1971. $6:50; paperback, $1.95.

The Water Lords. Edited by James Fallows. New York, Grossman, 1971. $7.95; paperback, $1.95.

Water Wasteland. Edited by David Zwick. New York, Grossman, 1971. $7.95; paperback $1.50.

The Closed Enterprise System: Ralph Nader's Study Group Report on Antitrust Enforcement. Edited by Mark J. Green. New York, Grossman, 1972. $8.95.

Sowing the Wind. Edited by Harrison Wellford. New York, Grossman, 1972. $7.95.

Politics of Land: Ralph Nader's Study Group Report on Land Use in California. Edited by Robert Fellmeth. New York, Grossman, 1972. $10.

The Company State: Ralph Nader's Study Group Report on Du Pont in Delaware. Edited by Robert Pozen and James Phelan. New York, Grossman, 1972. $7.95.

Damning the West: Ralph Nader's Study Group Report on the Bureau of Reclamation. Edited by Richard L. Berkman and Kip Viscusi. New York, Grossman, 1973. $7.95.

Tractor Safety Report. By James Williams. Washington, D.C., *Congressional Record,* September 17, 1969. $2.

Crash Safety in General Aviation Aircraft. Edited by James Bruce and John Draper. (Draft), 1970. $5.

H61 NATIONAL ASSOCIATION OF FOOD CHAINS 1725 Eye St., N.W., Washington, D.C. 20006 (Telephone: 202-338-7822).

The major function of the Association's Consumer Advisory Committee is to exchange information, experience, and ideas among its members so that each will perform effectively in communicating consumer desires and needs to company management and company action to the consumer.

H62 NATIONAL ASSOCIATION OF MANUFACTURERS (NAM) Marketing Committee, 277 Park Ave., New York, N.Y. 10017 (Telephone: 212-826-2100).

NAM's advice to consumers who feel frustrated because they get no response to their complaints is to "tell your story directly to the seller or the manufacturer." The leaflet, *The Concern for Quality*, offers step-by-step procedures that will help speed up the processing of complaints.

H63 NATIONAL ASSOCIATION OF RETAIL GROCERS OF THE U.S., INC. (NARGUS) 360 N. Michigan Ave., Chicago, Ill. 60601 (Telephone: 312-236-2107).

NARGUS offers two color, slide presentations of interest to consumers: "Consumer Beef Education Program" and "Consumer Pork Education Program." They explain meat cuts, products, and uses.

H64 NATIONAL AUTOMOBILE DEALERS ASSOCIATION 2000 K St., N.W., Washington, D.C. 20006.

H65 NATIONAL CANNERS ASSOCIATION (NCA) 1133 20th St., N.W., Washington, D.C. 20036 (Telephone: 202-338-2030).

Assurance of the quality and safety of canned foods through self-regulation is the aim of NCA. Its home economics-consumer service provides information on can and jar sizes, labeling, nutritive values, servings per container, and other up-to-date facts about canned foods. NCA publishes *The Canning Industry*; *Bibliography of Publications and Audio-Visual Aids*; and *Food Industry Sourcebook for Communication*.

H66 NATIONAL COMMISSION ON CONSUMER FINANCE 1016 16th St., N.W., Washington, D.C. 20036 (Telephone: 202-382-5634).

The Commission was created by Title IV of the Consumer Credit Protection Act of 1968 to "study and appraise the functioning and structure of the consumer finance industry, as well as consumer credit transactions generally" and to report to

Congress on: the adequacy of existing arrangements to provide consumer credit at reasonable rates; the adequacy of existing supervisory and regulatory mechanisms to protect the public from unfair practices and to ensure the informed use of consumer credit; and the desirability of federal chartering of consumer finance companies or other federal regulatory measures.

H67 **NATIONAL CONSUMER FINANCE ASSOCIATION** Suite 702, 1000 16th St., N.W., Washington, D.C. 20036 (Telephone: 202-638-1340).

The official trade association of the regulated consumer finance industry in the United States. Its activities include a research program, as well as educational and industry relations programs. Its Consumer Affairs Center handles inquiries and complaints from consumers about consumer credit. Its publications include *Family Budget Guide; Basic Principles in Family Money and Credit Management; Careers in Consumer Finance; Money and Your Marriage; Consumer Finance Industry; Consumer Finance News; Finance Facts; Consumer Finance Law Bulletin; Finance Facts Yearbook;* and *Selected and Annotated Bibliography of Reference Material in Consumer Finance.* A teacher's kit of materials on consumer finance is available, as well as a *Descriptive Catalog of Educational Materials for the Classroom Teacher or Counselor.*

H68 **NATIONAL CONSUMERS LEAGUE (NCL)** 1029 Vermont Ave., N.W., Washington, D.C. 20005 (Telephone: 202-347-3853).

NCL is an educational movement to awaken the interest of consumers to their responsibility for conditions under which goods are made and distributed and—through investigation, education, and legislation—to promote fair labor standards and the rights of consumers. NCL's monthly bulletin discusses current consumer topics.

H69 **NATIONAL COUNCIL ON THE AGING, INC. (NCOA)** 1828 L St., N.W., Washington, D.C. 20036.

The Council is a central, national resource for planning,

consultation, and publications devoted to a better life in later years. It keeps current with activities in the field; provides for interchange of information and ideas; presses for the training of professional personnel with competence in the field of aging; prepares books and pamphlets based on Council activities; summarizes and distributes reports of pertinent work of others; produces films, exhibits, and other visual aids; works with mass communication media to publicize programs and needs; provides field consultation within the limits of resources available; and carries on special projects, studies, and research under foundation and government grants and contracts. The Council maintains a library of printed materials with emphasis on the psychological, economic, and health aspects of aging. It publishes the quarterly *Current Literature on Aging* and the bimonthly newsletter, *NCOA Reports on the Aging*. A list of publications and audiovisual materials is available.

H70 **NATIONAL EDUCATION ASSOCIATION OF THE UNITED STATES (NEA)** 1201 16th St., N.W., Washington, D.C. 20036.

The *NEA Catalog* contains listings of NEA publishing units and their materials, with subject, title, and audiovisual indexes.

H71 **NATIONAL FOUNDATION FOR CONSUMER CREDIT, INC.** 1819 H St., N.W., Washington, D.C. 20006.

This nonprofit education and research organization is made up of the principal types of firms in 'the consumer credit field: retailers, bankers, consumer and sales finance institutions, credit bureaus, manufacturers, insurance companies, and other national organizations. Its objective is to provide the consumer with an understanding of credit and its uses through education, research, and counseling. Booklets available are: *Consumer Credit*; *The Forms of Credit We Use*; *Establishing Good Credit*; *Measuring and Using Our Credit Capacity*; and *The Emergency Problem, What to Do About It*.

H72 **NATIONAL INSTITUTE FOR CONSUMER JUSTICE**

Administrative Conference of the United States, 726 Jackson Pl., N.W., Washington, D.C. 20506.

This private, nonprofit corporation was formed in February 1971 to improve grievance-solving mechanisms and legal remedies for the consumer. The goal of the Institute is to develop basic information concerning the operation of the existing legal system as it affects consumers, especially the handling of small claims. In addition, the Institute will evaluate existing remedies and alternative private and public arrangements.

H73 **NATIONAL INSTITUTE OF DRYCLEANING** 909 Burlington Ave., Silver Spring, Md. 20910 (Telephone: 301-589-2334).

The Institute publishes the bimonthly *Fabric Facts Bulletin*, a quarterly *Clothing Care News*, a textbook on *Spotting*, and various brochures and leaflets. Its *Focus on Fabrics* contains definitions of fabric terms, finishes, construction, and dyeing and discusses types of fabrics, their selection, and care. *The Drycleaner and the Consumer* outlines types of services a drycleaner can and cannot provide. The Institute sponsors a correspondence course on "Fibers and Fabrics."

H74 **NATIONAL LEGAL AID AND DEFENDER ASSOCIATION (NLADA)** American Bar Center, 1155 E. 60th St., Chicago, Ill. 60637.

NLADA is a national coordinating and planning agency that provides local legal aid and defender assistance. Legal aid is defined as legal service—advice, negotiation, or assistance in court and before administrative agencies—for anyone who needs it, but cannot afford a private lawyer. People with questions should contact local legal aid services.

H75 **NATIONAL RESTAURANT ASSOCIATION** 1530 Lake Shore Dr., Chicago, Ill. 60610.

H76 **NATIONAL RETAIL MERCHANTS ASSOCIATION** 100 W. 31st St., New York, N.Y. 10001.

Economic Characteristics of Department Store Credit is available from this Association.

H77 NEIGHBORHOOD CLEANERS ASSOCIATION 116 E. 27th St., New York, N.Y. 10016.

H78 J.C. PENNEY COMPANY, INC. Educational and Consumer Relations Department, 1301 Avenue of the Americas, New York, N.Y. 10019.

Educational materials on use and care of major appliances, housing and home furnishings, textiles and clothing, color in fabrics, child development and family life, job opportunities, and consumer topics are available through local J.C. Penney stores.

H79 PETERSON COMPANY 8451 Melrose Ave., Hollywood, Calif. 90000.

"Before You Buy" is a course in consumer credit consisting of four cassette tapes, a student workbook, and teacher's manual.

H80 PHARMACEUTICAL MANUFACTURERS ASSOCIATION (PMA) 1155 15th St., N.W., Washington, D.C. 20005 (Telephone: 202-296-2440).

The active membership of this nonprofit, scientific, professional organization is comprised of approximately 130 firms principally engaged in the production of prescription drugs. Its objectives are to encourage high standards and research, to disseminate information, and to work with other professional groups in the health field. PMA publishes a brochure entitled *Key Facts About the U.S. Prescription Drug Industry.*

H81 PROCTOR AND GAMBLE COMPANY P.O. Box 14009, Cincinnati, Ohio 45214.

Several items are available: *Foods (Cake Selection)*; *Foods (Fats and Oils)*; *Laundering*; *Home Care*; *Personal Grooming*; and *Phosphates and Detergents.*

H82 PUBLIC AFFAIRS COMMITTEE, INC. 381 Park Ave., S., New York, N.Y. 10016 (Telephone: 212-683-4331).

The Committee is a nonprofit educational organization founded "to develop new techniques to educate the American public on vital economic and social problems and to issue concise and interesting pamphlets dealing with such problems." Five such pamphlets written by Sidney Margolius are: *How to S-t-r-e-t-c-h Your M-o-n-e-y* (No. 302A); *A Guide to Consumer Credit* (No. 348A); *How to Finance Your Home* (No. 360A); *Buyer, Be Wary* (No. 382); and *The Responsible Consumer* (No. 453). A list of additional pamphlets ($0.25 each) is available from the Committee.

H83   **SAFEWAY STORES, INC.**   6700 Columbia Park Rd., Landover, Md. 20785 (Telephone: 301-772-6900).

In addition to its unit pricing and open dating practices, this food chain offers food shopping tips, menu of the week, recipes, and educational leaflets on nutrition.

H84   **SEARS, ROEBUCK AND CO.**   303 E. Ohio St., Chicago, Ill. 60611.

Sears' Consumer Information Services offers many booklets in its *Hidden Values Series*. Included are: *How to Choose and Use Retail Credit; Your Space Age Kitchen; Fashions in Dining;* and *Let's Decorate the Bathroom*. In addition, there are seven *How to Select* titles: *Floor Coverings; Furniture; Infants' and Children's Clothing; Major Home Appliances; Paint and Wall Covering for Your Home; Window Treatments;* and *Young Underfashions.*

H85   **SOAP AND DETERGENT ASSOCIATION**   475 Park Ave., S., New York, N.Y. 10016 (Telephone: 212-725-1262).

The Association's consumer education services offer general consumer information and antipoverty program materials. Brochures are: *Dictionary of Cleanliness Products; Enzymes in Laundry Products; The Facts About Today's Detergents; Get Ready for Payday; Help Yourself; Beauty is Easy . . . At Any Age;* and *Housekeeping Directions* (also available in Spanish).

"Project Head Start" is an information packet to help instructors encourage preschool children to develop good health habits. "The Pursuit of Cleanliness" is an educational color film.

H86 SPECIAL ORGANIZATIONAL SERVICES (SOS) P.O. Box S.O.S., Athens, Tex. 75751 (Telephone: 214-675-7474).

SOS is a free, public service offered exclusively through banks to families of deceased persons. It is designed specifically to help survivors on such matters as the proper authorities to notify; immediate practical measures to be taken; and gathering basic information for claims in such areas as social security, civil service, veterans' benefits, railroad benefits, teachers' benefits, life insurance, credit life insurance, and profit-sharing plans.

H87 SUPER MARKET INSTITUTE, INC. (SMI) 200 E. Ontario St., Chicago, Ill. 60611 (Telephone: 312-664-4590).

The purpose of SMI is to improve the efficiency of grocery product distribution. It concentrates its efforts on the development of people, systems, and standards, and on the collection, organization, and dissemination of information about the distribution of grocery products. Its membership includes independent merchants, chain stores, and wholesalers. Although most of its materials are designed for members, two consumer education films are available—"The Price You Pay" and "Behind These Doors."

H88 UNDERWRITERS' LABORATORIES, INC. (UL) 207 E. Ohio St., Chicago, Ill., 60611.

Underwriters' Laboratories was founded in 1894 to establish, maintain, and operate laboratories for the investigation of materials, devices, products, equipment, constructions, methods, and systems with respect to hazards affecting life and property. UL's Consumer Advisory Council has the following responsibilities: to advise UL in establishing levels of safety for consumer products, to provide UL with additional user field experience and failure information in the area of product safety, and to aid in educating the general public in the limitations and safe use of specific consumer products. UL publishes the *Consumer Advisory Council Bulletin* which gives information to the ultimate consumer.

H89 WINN-DIXIE STORES, INC. 5050 Edgewood Court, P.O. Box B, Jacksonville, Fla. 32203 (Telephone: 904-384-5511).

This grocery chain has instituted unit pricing in its stores and offers a booklet, *Winn-Dixie's Consumer Guide.*

Index

Titles of publications which are main entries in the directory sections are indicated in all caps. Publication titles which appear within the description of a resource are in italics. Organizational resources are in initial caps only.

Subjects have been broken down into subheadings when it was deemed helpful to the user. In other cases, broad subject headings have been used.

DICTOCRATS, C41

Direct Mail Advertising Association, H35

Directories, E3, H7, pp. 4-19

Director of Consumer Affairs (Florida), F70

DIRECTORY OF AMERICAN SAVINGS AND LOAN ASSOCIATIONS, A23

DIRECTORY OF GOVERNMENT AGENCIES SAFEGUARDING CONSUMER AND ENVIRONMENT, A24

DIRECTORY OF INFORMATION RESOURCES IN AGRICULTURE AND BIOLOGY, A25

A DIRECTORY OF INFORMATION RESOURCES IN THE UNITED STATES, A26

DIRECTORY OF LEGAL AID AND DEFENDER SERVICES, 1971, A27

DIRECTORY OF SPECIAL LIBRARIES AND INFORMATION CENTERS, A28

A *Directory of State Officials Charged with the Enforcement of Food, Drug, Cosmetic, and Food Laws*, E11

DIRECTORY OF URBAN AFFAIRS INFORMATION AND RESEARCH CENTERS, A29

District of Columbia, C101, p. 87

Division of Consumer Affairs (Delaware), F56

Division of Consumer Affairs, Department of Law and Public Safety, State of New Jersey, F173

Division of Consumer Affairs, Department of Public Safety (Florida), F65

Division of Consumer Affairs, Department of Weights and Measures, Ventura County (California), F22

Division of Consumer Services, Florida Department of Agriculture and Consumer Services, F72

Division of Home Economics—Federal Extension Service, USDA, E3

Division of Weights and Measures and

Consumer Affairs (Kentucky), F114

Doak, Wesley A., A35

Doctors, C12, C17, C93

Dollars and Decisions, F260

THE DOLLAR SQUEEZE AND HOW TO BEAT IT, C42

Dolphin, Robert, Jr., B22

Don't Be Gypped, E10

DON'T YOU BELIEVE IT, C43

The Door to Door Selling Law, F53

DOT, *see* U.S. Department of Transportation

Dowd, Merle E., C67

Dow Jones & Company, Inc., H36

Downtown Business Association Consumers Bureau, F12

Doyle, Patrick J., C93

Draper, John, H60

DRUG & COSMETIC INDUSTRY, D34

Drugs, A24, A50, A62, C8, C10, C11, C61, C92, C93, C103, D30, D34, E11, E13, F51, H80, pp. 94, 97, 100, 119, 121

The Drycleaner and the Consumer, H73

DUN'S REVIEW, D43

ECONOMIC ALMANAC, C44

Economic Characteristics of Department Store Credit, H76

Economics, B4, B5, B11, B13, C44

ECONOMICS FOR CONSUMERS, B11

THE ECONOMICS OF TRADING STAMPS, C45

EDUCATIONAL MEDIA INDEX, A30

Education Directory, E19

EDUCATION INDEX, A31

Effect of DOD Directive No. 1344.7 on Creditors Bordering Fort Riley, F105

Elderly, C7, H69

El Use Del Credito, F53

The Emergency Problem, What to Do About It, H71

ENCYCLOPEDIA OF ASSOCIATIONS, A32